D1384440

LADY OF THE DANCE

First published 2017 by The O'Brien Press Ltd,
12 Terenure Road East, Rathgar, Dublin 6, D06 HD27, Ireland.
Tel: +353 1 4923333; Fax: +353 1 4922777
E-mail: books@obrien.ie. Website: www.obrien.ie
The O'Brien Press is a member of Publishing Ireland.

ISBN: 978-1-84717-926-5

8 7 6 5 4 3 2 1
21 20 19 18 17

Printed and bound by Scandbook AB, Sweden
The paper used in this book is produced using pulp from managed forests.

The author and publisher thank the following for permission to use
photographs and illustrative material: Photo section one, page 7 (bottom)
and photo section two, page 2 (bottom) courtesy of Brian McEvoy. Photo
section two, page 1 (bottom right) courtesy of Rita Wood of Amber Wood
Photography. All other images are from the author's personal collection or
courtesy of Michael Flatley and *Lord of the Dance*.

Published in

DUBLIN
UNESCO
City of Literature

LADY

OF THE

DANCE

MARIE DUFFY
WITH EDDIE ROWLEY

THE O'BRIEN PRESS
DUBLIN

DEDICATION

To my mother

ACKNOWLEDGEMENTS

In my life I've been blessed with great people who've been there for me through the good times, but especially when the going got tough. It has not been possible to mention every one of you by name in the telling of my story, but you know who you are and you will always be in my heart.

I have had many 'families' as you will discover. I was lucky to be reared in a great family with a lovely gang of brothers and by a mother who had big dreams for me. I hope she's smiling down today.

I will always remember the Maoileidgh family with affection, and the wonderful families and friends I have met through the Irish dance community and CLRG.

I have been lucky in love twice – the first time with my late husband Ian Messenger, and I'd like to thank Ian's family for their love and support.

My dear friends James and Noreen McCutcheon, Hilary Joyce Owens and Barry Owens have put in countless hours keeping me afloat during difficult times in recent years.

Words can't describe how much I appreciate and value the support and friendship of Eben Foggitt and his wife, Sharon, and particularly their selfless service to The Marie Duffy Foundation.

I've lived a very fulfilled life through Irish dance, and I never imagined that I would end up working on one of the biggest dance shows in the world. A phone call from Michael Flatley changed my life. Michael, I will never forget the opportunity you gave me to have the most incredible experiences around the globe. Thank you for the laughs, tears, dramas and thrills. But above all, thank you for your friendship, Michael and Niamh.

To everyone involved in *Lord of the Dance* – what an adventure that has been for all of us! I hope I've done it justice between the covers of this book.

Here I would like to thank my co-writer, Eddie Rowley, author and show-biz editor of the *Sunday World*, who helped me put the jigsaw of my life together. My heartfelt thanks also to Eddie's wife, Patricia, for the hours spent transcribing my recordings.

Thank you to Patrick O'Donoghue and the staff at the former Columba Press for their early work on this book. To Michael O'Brien and the staff of The O'Brien Press, my sincere thanks for bringing it to life and for a beautiful production.

Last but not least, to my husband, Mike Pask, and his gorgeous family. I don't know what I would do without Mike in my life. He is the most incredible man, as you will learn in my story. Thank you Mike for your unconditional love, particularly during very challenging times. You know I adore you.

CONTENTS

by Michael Flatley

Marie Duffy is a legend.

Her dedication to the teaching and development of Irish dance from an early age has been a driving force of the Irish Dancing Commission on a global scale.

Her relentless optimism in times when seemingly insurmountable hurdles have presented themselves has been an inspiration to all who have worked with her.

I have known Marie as close as a 'sister' for more than twenty years and known of her reputation for even longer.

It was that reputation as a driven and motivated teacher, choreographer and promoter of Irish dance that made Marie Duffy the only person I could choose to help realise my vision for *Lord of the Dance*.

Over the years Marie trained countless world champions and her attention to detail and perfectionism is something we connected on right from the start.

Marie has never been afraid to push the boundaries; and when we first met and I told her my ideas she never faltered or said that it can't be done, but immediately jumped on board.

It was that kind of positivity and can-do attitude that I needed in a time when, for me, my dreams had just been torn apart.

We made history in the world of Irish dance in such a positive way.

We have been on an incredible journey and have had many highs and lows, from magnificent opening nights to last-minute crises that tested our strength, but there has never been a time when I didn't have Marie Duffy by my side.

We laughed and we cried together and worked endless hours together in the pursuit of perfection.

She has been a best friend and will always remain so.

She has been unquestionably loyal to me and *Lord of the Dance* throughout all of my shows, from the beginning and on to *Feet of Flames*, *Celtic Tiger* and most recently *Lord of the Dance: Dangerous Games* – not to mention the many other TV shows and special one-off performances for royalty and heads of state around the world.

In fact if you looked up the word 'loyal' in the dictionary I am pretty sure there would be a picture of Marie Duffy beside it.

It was a sad and poignant moment in 2015 when she came onstage with me to take her final bow on Broadway, marking her retirement. A more fitting or worthy stage for the lady who worked her way to the top from the basement of a small, run-down dance hall in Dublin city there could not have been.

Marie has left an indelible mark not only on me, but on the hundreds of dancers that have come through our doors.

And although she has retired I know she is always just a phone call away.

I love Marie and am proud of her.

She is one in a million.

DANCING THROUGH LIFE

Welcome to Hollywood.

It's March 1997 and I'm at the Oscars with Michael Flatley and the *Lord of the Dance* troupe.

It's a 'pinch yourself' moment for me – a long way from my humble upbringing in Crumlin, Dublin.

Flying on Russian president Vladimir Putin's private plane is also a long way from Crumlin. But that's another story.

'Dream big and make it happen,' Michael Flatley used to say.

The Oscars were never in my dreams. But I've had the privilege of helping Michael stage the spectacular *Lord of the Dance* show from scratch and this is where the journey has taken me.

I had lived my entire life in the world of Irish dance. Then in middle age I went into semi-retirement.

It was a phone call from Michael Flatley that brought me back. And this time my platform would be the world stage in one of the greatest dance productions ever seen.

It wasn't all glamour and excitement along the way, of course, as we battled the clock to launch *Lord of the Dance*. Yes we had a lot of fun, but we worked all the hours that God sent to get the show up and, well, dancing.

'We didn't come this far to finish second,' Michael would say during our tough times in those early days.

We put dance teams of young men and women together, and taught and drilled them until we had a world-class show.

Then Michael stepped out front and created his magic, performing the Irish steps like no one else on earth.

Finally it was time to lift the curtain and show the universe what we had to offer. *Lord of the Dance* became an instant success with both the fans and the critics.

And now here I am backstage at the Oscars, among all the fuss and glitter and glam of this greatest showbiz night of the year in Los Angeles.

I'm rubbing shoulders with some of the most famous names in Hollywood. I've seen the diminutive but very handsome Tom Cruise stroll by, charming all the ladies with his gorgeous smile.

Then along comes Ralph Fiennes, who put poor Mr Cruise in the shade. With his sexy, smouldering good looks, it's this gorgeous Englishman who creates knee trembles. At this moment Ralph is the toast of Hollywood thanks to his amazing performance in *The English Patient*.

How I ended up at this incredible night in the world of entertainment is just part of the story of my life.

Here in Hollywood the moviemakers love a rags-to-riches, success against all odds personal drama.

To make it all the way to the Oscars in Hollywood is a script I would never have written for myself – coming, as I have done, from Ireland of the 1940s and 1950s when families like mine had little or no money and struggled to make ends meet.

Now I'm thinking of my mother, who put me on the path that has taken me to Hollywood. When she scraped together the cash for my Irish dancing classes as a child, she could never have foreseen where that would take me in life.

If only she was here in Los Angeles to witness this night unfold.

What has happened to me shows that you're never too old to follow your dream or take on a challenge.

How I ended up here in my middle age is a story full of twists and turns.

But little did I know that shortly after this momentous night at the Oscars a tragic event with devastating consequences was about to destroy my happiness.

There is a cruel side to life.

Thankfully, though, what life takes it sometimes gives back and I would be granted that gift.

That's life and all its mysteries.

And the story of my life begins on Cashel Road, Crumlin, Dublin, in the 1940s ...

A SURPRISE CHILD

My mother Mary, God rest her, had notions about me as a child.

We never discussed it in adult life, but today as I journey back into my childhood I can see that she was doing her best to raise me, her youngest child and only surviving daughter, as a little lady.

Maybe she was blinded by her good intentions, but Mother didn't realise that the road she put me on left me feeling sad, lonely and insecure as I grew up.

I lived my young life without a circle of friends, and, sad to recall, I didn't have a lot of carefree fun. It was all so different for the boys: my brothers and their friends on the street. I'd press my face up against the window of the front room in our modest terraced house and stare with envy and longing at the noisy gang of boys laughing and screaming as they were swinging from ropes tied to street lamp posts, or playing a game of hopscotch.

It was simple, harmless fun, but I couldn't go there. I guess my mother thought that the street playground was too common for her little lady.

* * *

There were seven boys in my family, but alongside the births of those seven brothers there were also three girls – my sisters who didn't survive. One of them was a twin of my youngest brother, Brian. I can't imagine the trauma that my parents, and particularly my mother, must have suffered losing their baby girls.

It's no wonder, then, that she wrapped me in cotton wool when I came into the world.

I was the surprise pregnancy in my parents' marriage, and I was born seven years after their last surviving child, Brian. By then, they had most of their children reared. Three of my brothers, Owen, Joe and Michael, had already left home and were out in the big bad world fending for themselves.

Mother was then looking after four young sons, Kevin, Tony, Seamas and Brian ... and along comes a baby daughter.

The shock of the pregnancy for my mother must have been eased by the arrival of a healthy baby girl when I came into the world on 8 December 1945.

But if there was any joy in a daughter arriving into her life Mother didn't get to savour the moment, because she took ill after the birth.

The district midwife who delivered me in the bedroom of our neat two-up, two-down corporation house at 213 Cashel Road in the working-class Crumlin suburb of Dublin city, was my mother's sister, Emily, who was also chosen as my godmother.

My auntie Emily, or Aunt Em as she was known in our clan, was a tiny woman with a formidable personality, and she would become a major presence in my life during the years that followed. She was my mother's backbone really, as she was very supportive of her throughout her life. She dominated my mother, but in a good way.

Aunt Em was married and had one son, Tom, who was the same age as my brother Brian.

My mother was in her forties when she gave birth to me, and in those days women rarely had babies at that age because the risks were so high. They got married young, had a child year after year, and were grandmothers in their forties. My mother paid the price for giving birth so late in her life. When I was born she was in a lot of physical distress and became so ill that she was finally admitted into hospital, where tests showed that she was suffering from kidney failure and other issues.

Aunt Em then stepped up to her responsibilities as a godmother by taking me on while my poor mother recovered. She brought me over to her home in Artane on the north side of the city, much to the delight of her seven-year-old only child, Tom. By all accounts, it was the best Christmas ever for young Tom, because his house came alive with the arrival of baby Marie.

God love him, I think Tom thought I was there to stay forever. He doted on me, according to the family. Gradually, my mother got better and was well enough to be reunited with me at home. And I don't think anyone expected the impact it would have on young Tom when he discovered that the baby was leaving.

On the day my mother arrived for me, Tom became hysterical.

He grabbed at her clothing, screaming, 'You can't take the baby, she's ours!'

Poor Tom, he was inconsolable.

'Marie's my sister, she's my sister, she has to stay here!' he cried and cried.

My mother said her heart went out to the youngster, but sure what could she do?

Poor Tom.

Back home, my mother realised that she really wasn't well enough to cope with four boisterous young boys and a baby. But rather than send me back to Aunt Em she asked my newly married brother Joe, and his wife Elizabeth, or Bett as she was known, to come home from England to look after me for a few months.

It was good training for them: nine months later, Joe and Bett became parents themselves when my nephew, David, was born.

Before I was born, my mother had chosen the name Philomena if her child turned out to be a girl. But because my arrival into the world was on the Feast of the Immaculate Conception, a day that celebrates the solemn belief in the Immaculate Conception of the Blessed Virgin Mary, being a good Catholic my mother called me Marie Philomena.

At first she had pronounced my name Ma-*ree*, with the emphasis on the 'ree'. So all my brothers and other family members got to know me as Ma-*ree*.

Then a few months later a daughter was born into the Nolan family who lived down the road. And they called her Marie, pronounced Ma-*ree*. Well, my mother was raging. So, from then on she insisted that my name should now be pronounced *Mar*-ee, with a strong 'ah'.

By then, of course, my siblings had got used to calling me Ma-*ree*, so that's how they addressed me all their lives. But to my mother, I would always be *Mar*-ee.

I have no idea what that was all about, but I guess she was snobbish in her own peculiar way.

* * *

Cashel Road is a long road and is in two parts. In our section, there were five houses in each block and they were all full of boys of a similar age. Then over-night a girl appeared in two of them: our house and in our neighbours' next door. The Tynan family also welcomed the arrival of their baby daughter, Beryl, around the same time that I was born.

For a long time in my childhood, Beryl would be my only friend. Like myself, Beryl wasn't allowed out to play street games with the boys. So we just had our own company, and sometimes we would both peer longingly out the window at the boys and be so envious of all the fun they were having with the variety of games they invented. Beryl and I would always have a bond in life, but we didn't see a lot of each other after I started school at the age of six.

When it came to my education, my mother had lofty ideas. Not for me the local convent school, St Agnes's, at the end of our road in Crumlin. Instead, Mother got me enrolled in the Presentation Convent in the more affluent suburb of Terenure.

I presume she believed that being educated at a school in Terenure would help me to achieve a greater status in life, or perhaps land me a better position in the workplace in the years ahead.

My young friend, Beryl, meanwhile, was sent to an Irish language school in the city. As time would tell, that school was probably more suited to my needs since I ended up steeped in Irish culture and dancing, but I struggled with the language.

In order to qualify for a place in the Presentation College, you had to be residing in Terenure. This was just a minor detail that my mother resolved with little difficulty. Her brother, Michael O'Kelly, lived at 8 Parkmore Drive in the area, so she used his address to get me into the school.

I didn't stay with my uncle Michael. Instead I would do a daily commute to Terenure on the 82 bus, which stopped at the end of our road. This left me alienated as a child, as now I didn't have friends in either Crumlin or in Terenure.

The kids who went to St Agnes's all played together after school, and the pupils in the Terenure area had their own little groups where they lived.

Meanwhile, I was commuting by bus between both suburbs, so I didn't get the chance to have friends in either community.

I became an outsider, which is a lonely place to be, particularly as a child. I didn't even have Beryl around at the weekends. She was in a similar situation to me – not having local friends – because she went to a school outside our area.

At this stage, Beryl and I went in totally different directions when she began spending weekends with her cousins on the other side of the city.

My mother no doubt thought she was doing her best by me, but she could have started me in school earlier. I was half reared when I entered the Presentation Convent at the age of six and, probably since I'd had very little interaction with other children up to that point, I was incredibly quiet and introverted.

To get me to speak was really hard. I had so many disadvantages starting out in the education system, not least being the fact that the other children in my class had settled in to their daily routine six months ahead of me.

Mother sent me to school on my sixth birthday, which fell in the month of December, so I was a long way behind the rest of the class who'd been there since the end of the summer holidays.

I had a lot of catching up to do.

On my first day in the school, the nun who was teaching us began by reading out everyone's name from a book. I would later learn that this was the roll call. As each child answered, I thought they said, 'I'm sorry.'

When I heard my name called out I stayed silent, because as far as I was concerned I had nothing to be sorry about. The nun moved on to another name. This happened over a couple of days until the nun eventually realised that I was in the room but not responding.

'Will somebody answer for that child,' she roared.

Then one girl nudged me with a bony elbow and whispered, 'Say "anseo"!'

I had no idea what that was. It would be some time before the message got through to me.

What I was hearing was not 'I'm sorry', but the Irish word 'anseo', meaning present or here.

I hadn't learned any Irish at that stage and had obviously missed all the introductory instruction in the class six months earlier.

The nuns and teachers in the Presentation College were quite tough and strict at the time. I didn't embrace school life because I simply didn't like it. Any chance I got, I would have an excuse to avoid going into school.

Strangely, my mother aided and abetted me. She allowed me to stay at home quite a lot. As the only girl and the last child, I guess she liked having me around the house.

Of course, there was a price to be paid for my truancy.

When the time came for me to go into third class, the nun in charge took four of us aside and dropped the bombshell: we were being held back to repeat second class again.

I was devastated and immediately burst into tears. I'm sure you could have heard me wailing all over the school, and the other three were no better. We were like an out of tune choral group.

Needless to say, there was no sympathy from the nun. 'What do you expect with the amount of time you've missed?' she sternly announced.

The wiry old nun, with a voice that would pierce your ears, was right of course, but I felt ill with the shame of being kept back a year. However, after I recovered from the shock it dawned on me, even at that young age, that in order to achieve you have to be dedicated to what you're doing, and you have to work hard at it.

That day changed my life. As I looked to the future, I was determined that I was going to be the best in my class. I resolved to listen and learn, and to study whatever came my way.

Without realising it, I used the hurt and disgrace I felt that day as motivation to make the most of any opportunity that came my way throughout my life.

I got a hunger for learning.

I'd learnt my lesson, and I hardly ever missed a day in school again.

MY DAD TOOK A BULLET

My father often told me that I came at the wrong end of the family. By then, Dad was battling through very poor health – even to this day I can still hear the terrible cough that afflicted him – and struggling to make a decent living. I think it troubled Dad greatly that he wasn't in a position to provide me with the material things of life. But that beautiful man, Joe Duffy, probably didn't realise he was giving me the greatest gifts of all: love and security.

I always felt loved by my father, even though he wasn't a tactile sort of person. In those times most men didn't hug and kiss their children or spend endless amounts of time playing with them like the young fathers of today. Well, at least my dad didn't. He wasn't very hands-on, but I guess his bad health had a lot to do with that as well.

Dad had a very colourful life behind him by the time I came into his world, not least due to his active role as a volunteer fighter during the Irish War of Independence. This led to him being wounded during a major event in Irish history: the burning of the Custom House in Dublin on 25 May 1921. The Custom House was then the centre of local government in the British administration in Ireland. The Irish Republican Army occupied and burnt it in an operation that involved over 100 volunteers, including my father.

Dad was shot in a lane around the Liberty Hall area as he was running away from the scene.

While he survived the shooting, the bullet lodged close to his ribs and couldn't be removed, so he carried it around for the rest of his life.

Both sides of my family were active in the War of Independence. My uncle, Michael O'Kelly, was a Lieutenant Colonel in E. Company, 2nd Battalion of the Dublin Brigade of the Irish Republican Army, and also played an active role in the burning of the Custom House. He was captured and sentenced to death, but was later released from prison after the signing of the Treaty.

When I knew him, Uncle Michael, who had two children, Maurice and June, was living at Parkmore Drive in Terenure, which, as I mentioned, is the address my mother used to get me into the local convent school.

I'm told that my grandfather, Joseph O'Kelly, was also a personal bodyguard to Michael Collins. My mother, who was a middle child, had five brothers and five sisters, and I think that most of them played some role in the struggle and received medals for their service. I remember hearing them tell stories about the Black and Tans – as the British soldiers were called because of their uniforms – and how they came raiding houses in the Drumcondra area of Dublin. My aunts were running from house to house raising the alarm to get their brothers safely out of the district. They raided my grandfather's house on Carlton Road, smashing the piano and pulling up floorboards looking for arms.

Aunt Em is also famous in the family for playing her part in fighting the old enemy. Legend has it that she knew how to handle a gun and took out a few of them in her time, but she never owned up to it. Aunt Em had quite a reputation; although she was four-foot-nothing you'd be terrified to cross her.

Later in life I would hear stories about Aunt Em attending gatherings of the Old IRA. On those occasions the men would assemble in one room, while the women got together separately. However, Aunt Em was always invited to join the men, and was exceptionally popular among them. One of my relatives informed me that this was because she had been 'a shooter' for the Irish Republican Army, 'and those men were glad to have Emily covering their backs at the time'.

Both my father and mother were awarded medals for their service with the Irish Volunteers during that turbulent period. And my father received a disability allowance for his injury.

That injury, however, changed the course of Dad's life, and probably my own. I remember my brother Tony recalling one time that my father wanted to emigrate to Australia and take the whole family Down Under. This would have been before I was born. However, Dad failed his medical test, which meant he wasn't allowed to become a resident in Australia, where, otherwise, I might have been born and reared. Tony said he felt there was a great change in my father after that. He became very quiet in the house.

Growing up I was always aware of the fact that Dad was exceptionally popular among the people in our area. It seemed to me that everybody loved Joe Duffy. My impression is that they thought my mum was the hard one in the relationship, but, as I explained, she had to run the home and keep the boys in check. My mother did the ruling and barked out the orders, and you obeyed her.

I remember my dad being a quiet, gentle man with a head of lush silver hair. He was of average height, but very thin. Although he had done his bit for Irish independence, my recollection of him is that he was a frail man, so it is hard for me to envisage Dad as a freedom fighter or soldier back in the day.

My parents continued to be active in politics and were supporters of Fine Gael, with Dad becoming secretary of the local branch. During election time our house would be full of propaganda leaflets of every shape and size. You couldn't see out the windows of our home due to the billboards that were plastered all over them, shutting out the light and the world outside.

Although my mother supported Fine Gael, it drove her mad when party workers would take over her house and use it as their centre of operations. And when they got into full canvassing mode you'd think we had a revolving door with the number of people arriving in to pick up or drop off their electioneering paraphernalia.

I remember one of the Fine Gael luminaries at that time was a guy called Richie Ryan. Later, as the Minister for Finance in the crisis years of the Irish economy between 1973 and 1977, he was lampooned on the satirical *Hall's Pictorial Weekly* TV show in Ireland. They called him 'Richie Ruin, the Minister for Hardship', because of the savage taxes he introduced as his government struggled to sort out the nation's financial woes. Richie spent a lot of time in our house plotting his campaign the first time he went up for election.

As there was nobody to mind me when my mum and dad went out canvassing for the Fine Gael candidates, I tagged along, hanging on to their coat tails. Then election days were spent in the polling hall with them; I would always be so bored having to hang around from early morning till late at night. My father really was very dedicated to the party and spent a lot of time as a general dogsbody for them for no personal gain whatsoever, as it was voluntary work. His loyalty was all the more commendable when you consider the fact that he had the constant worry of finding work to support us.

For many years after I was born, I slept in my parents' bedroom with them. The four remaining boys were in the second room. But I recall one time my father emigrated to England in search of work, leaving us behind. The older brothers who had left home were already working in different factories there, so they always found a job for him. And I missed him terribly when he was away.

When he returned home, I remember him being sick quite a lot with infections. But Dad was a worker and provider and he pushed on, taking whatever employment that came along.

When I was about ten years of age, he got a job as a night watchman on a building site during the construction of corporation houses in the Ballyfermot area of Dublin. Around seven in the evening I would set off with my mother, taking a couple of bus rides over to the buildings to bring him his supper. I'll never forget the sadness I felt on dark nights with the rain pouring down, seeing Dad all alone in the little hut on the eerie expanse of land amidst the shells of half-built houses, and then leaving him there all night on his own when we returned home. It was heartbreaking to witness the life he lived as a worker and the hardship he endured.

The last day of the month is etched in my memory because that's when Dad would get his disability pension. I'd go with my mum to meet him when he got the cash, so that she'd get her monthly allowance. Mum knew that Dad was a soft touch and he'd have plenty of so-called friends to help him spend his earnings in the pub. Then there was the danger that we'd be left with nothing for the rest of the month. He was a very generous man; he'd give away every penny he had.

Like the other men in the area, my father's only leisure activity was a trip to the local pubs whenever he could afford it. He went for companionship rather than to get drunk.

When I was a child we had a mongrel dog called Tiny, so called because he was so little. Tiny was very attached to my father and would tag along with him wherever he went, including on his occasional outings to the local bars. Whenever we wanted to find Dad all we had to do was go on a little trip from pub to pub until we came to the one with Tiny sitting outside, waiting patiently for his master to emerge. There was no hiding place for Dad with that lovable, miniature hairy mutt giving the game away.

* * *

I'm sure my parents really felt the pressure of their dire financial circumstances when Christmas came around. There were no jingle bells or glitter in my childhood during that festive season. Our Christmases were very frugal. You never wrote to Santa asking for a particular toy or present; you just hoped that he'd bring you something, and you took what you got without complaint.

Sometimes Santa would come up trumps. One toy I remember being thrilled with was a tiny doll's pram that said 'Mama!' when you pressed the handles. That was a very unusual present for the times that were in it.

However, there were often times when Santa left me feeling disappointed and sad. One of those years was when we spent Christmas at my brother Joe and his wife Bett's home in the English town of Didcot, Oxfordshire. My father had been working there in a factory with my brother, so my mother took us over to join him for Christmas. On Christmas Day I opened my present from Santa and found a tiny easel and stand, which was only a foot high. My nephews and nieces, who were close in age to me, got much more exciting toys. I couldn't take my eyes off their gifts and I was so envious, but I didn't dare complain. Inside, I felt like crying, but I put on a brave face. Then my sister-in-law, Bett, gave me a present that brought a huge smile to my face. It was a sewing set. I thought it was the bee's knees and I treasured it for years and years afterwards.

My brothers and their wives were very good to me as a child. One time when Tony, who lived in Harlesden, London, went into the army in England to do his two years' compulsory service and was away in Singapore, we minded his child, Joan. She had so many lovely toys. I took a shine to a gorgeous bridal doll that was one of many she owned. Joan's mother Lena spotted my fascination with the beautiful doll and she persuaded Joan to give her to me as a gift. I was absolutely thrilled, and that doll became a childhood treasure that I took with me into my adult life.

I don't recall ever seeing a roast turkey on our table at Christmas. Instead, it would be a chicken dinner. One time, when we were really hard up, Aunt Em invited us over to her home for a festive meal. There were just my parents and myself living at home at the time. For some reason that I never discovered, my father had an issue with this and refused to go. Perhaps he felt embarrassed that he couldn't provide for us and didn't want to take Aunt Em's charity. He was a very proud man in his own way. I heard my mother arguing with him, saying, 'Well, I don't have any money to get Christmas food in.'

There was no talking to my father. He just wouldn't come with us. So my mother and myself deserted him that Christmas Day as we headed off to Aunt Em's for our feast. I was really upset leaving my poor old dote of a dad at home alone and without a decent meal to celebrate that special day of the year.

Despite Aunt Em's hospitality and generosity, I didn't enjoy a moment of the get-together or the lovely spread she laid on for us that Christmas.

I couldn't stop thinking about my father being alone.

I just wanted to be with him – food or no food I didn't really care.

The heartbreak of that Christmas Day has always stayed with me.

THE COMMUNION DRESS

My little heart beat wildly against my chest as the white dress was lowered over my head.

Long before the fairy-tale wedding of every woman's dream, first holy communion was a girl's first love affair with an iconic dress. Even though we were just seven years old, it was the centre of our world in the weeks leading up to the day we would receive the sacrament of Holy Communion for the very first time. Thoughts of the formalities around that religious ceremony in the church scared me, but I just couldn't wait for my amazing dress.

My mother slipped the creation down over my body, tucked it in here and there, and gently slid up the zip at the back. Then I turned around and I felt like I was going to faint with excitement as I skipped over to the full-length mirror to admire what I imagined to be this most beautiful of beautiful dresses that my mother had engaged a local dressmaker to make for me.

I almost burst into floods of tears when I saw my reflection in the mirror. To my young eyes, the dress was a disaster. It was ragged and uneven; too high on one side, too low on the other. My mother was still doing her best to beat it into shape as she tugged and pulled at it, but the magic was gone for me. I didn't let on to her how upset I felt over this huge letdown, but I'm sure Mum could see through my feeble attempt to conceal my feelings.

On the morning of my first holy communion she tried to reassure me that I looked like a little princess. I smiled and hugged her, and then I nervously slipped away to join the army of girls in white before we paraded up the aisle of St Joseph's Church in Terenure.

I was mortified and I didn't dare glance at the faces of people in the congregation that morning because I felt they were all staring at my inferior dress that dipped below my coat. Even a coat couldn't hide all its imperfections. There was no doubt in my mind that they were feeling sorry for the poor child that was wearing it.

As if I didn't have enough insecurities at that time.

I'm certain that my mother was equally upset over my first communion dress, but there was nothing she could do; we just didn't have the money to change it. When I made my confirmation several years later, I was really pleased with the outfit I got for that occasion. This time my mother had done forward planning for it, joining one of those savings clubs where you put money in over a period of time to buy an outfit. I was even allowed to choose the dress I wore that day.

* * *

My mother had a great sense of style, as I would come to appreciate when I got older, and there was a little bit more cash to go around. She never had money to splash out on new clothes, but she would take a trip to the best second-hand shops, or the markets in town, and sift through them until she found the most unusual, beautiful items for both of us. I inherited my mother's passion for clothes and fashion, and I do believe I picked up her flair and talent for mixing and matching outfits.

Mother was also passionate about Irish culture.

Although we were poor and just getting by like everybody else in the neighbourhood (and probably the entire country), she gave us the opportunity to learn music and dancing.

Shortly after I started school she organised piano lessons for me with a teacher called Johnny Fox, who gave classes at his home on Sundrive Road in our area. I joined a group of other young children around my own age, and we'd sit on stools peppered around Johnny's parlour as we waited our turn.

I would be sick with nerves as I sat rigid on the wooden stool listening to each pupil murdering some tune. Then I'd be completely overcome with terror when my moment came to step over to the piano, as everyone else in the little room watched and listened to the torture that I inflicted on the poor instrument.

Next came Irish dancing – and my mother could never have foreseen where that was going to take me in life. Seamas and Brian were the first to take up the dancing after it was introduced in their school, which was run by the Christian Brothers and located at the end of our road.

The Irish dancing teacher who ran classes there after school hours was a man called Maitiu Ó Maoiléidigh, or Matt Meleady. While Brian showed early promise as a dancer and soon developed a love for it, Seamas had little interest.

And if Seamas wasn't interested in something, wild horses wouldn't drag him to it.

When Matt Meleady organised a céilí dance, Seamas decided to make his statement about what he thought of those Irish dancing shenanigans. Seamas didn't go to the dance alone. Full of devilment, he brought along his little pet … a white mouse. Then he waited for the moment he felt would have maximum impact, and let the mouse loose on the floor.

The tiny creature caused pandemonium when it was spotted by the girls as it scurried around amongst the feet of the dancers. Seamas fell around the place laughing at the chaos that ensued, and was promptly kicked out of dancing class forever.

Brian, on the other hand, took a real shine to the dancing, as did a couple of his mates on the road. Matt spotted Brian's skill and encouraged him to join Craobh an Chéitinnigh, a class he ran for senior dancers at the Gaelic League headquarters over at 46 Parnell Square in the city centre.

I recall being very excited when Brian went on to take part in the All-Ireland competitions. Even though I was only seven at the time, I was conscious of the fact that this was a huge event for Brian to be involved in. I could see that my mother was very proud of him, and we all went to the train station to wave him off with the rest of the troupe of dancers.

Their destination that day was Belfast, where the All-Ireland dancing competitions were being held for the very first time outside Dublin. We were back at the train station again for their big homecoming, and they were all dripping with medals after doing exceptionally well in the various categories.

The following week Mum asked Brian to give his dancing teacher a message. She wanted the instructor to call by our house, which he duly did. When he arrived there was some small talk, and then my mother introduced me and told this stranger how much I enjoyed Irish music, and how I wanted to learn to dance. 'Marie, play a tune for the man,' my mother said, shooing me over to the piano. Even though I was mortified, I obliged.

The teacher politely applauded and was very complimentary when I finished. This gave my mother the opportunity to mention the real reason she had requested him to call in.

She asked if I could join Matt's dancing class. What could the poor man say only 'yes'?

My journey into the world of Irish dancing began at the tender age of seven in Matt Meleady's class of junior dancers. Craobh an Chéitinnigh were the senior dancers, so Matt called his junior class Inis Ealga.

Of course, I was terrified starting off, joining all the other children in the beginner's class. One of the older dancers, a chap called Patrick Elebert, taught me my first steps, the side step and one, two, three.

I settled in very quickly because I was enjoying it, but it would be a long time before I became proficient at Irish dancing and won some awards.

Despite his early success as a dancer, Brian eventually lost interest and gave it up. Seamas, meanwhile, was also on the move – out of school.

Even though he was very bright, Seamas had no interest in the academic life. My mother had a terrible time trying to get him to go to school and he was missing more often than he was there. Eventually the principal of the Christian Brothers School called my mother in to discuss his future.

Seamas had expressed an interest in becoming a chef, so the school principal said, 'If he gets an apprenticeship let him take it up because that's obviously where his heart lies.'

Not long afterwards Seamas left school at the age of thirteen and began his training as a chef.

Seamas was definitely the character in our family. He was tall, slim, handsome and very outgoing, with a wicked sense of humour, as the incident with the pet mouse would tell you. Later I would think how Seamas reminded me of the singer Frank Sinatra. He had Sinatra's manner and the same bold, cheeky personality.

My mother obviously doted on Seamas and did little to curb his wild ways as a teenager. He was the only one in the family who got away with using the f-word in the house. Mother might frown or give him a dirty look if he was using bad language, but Seamas would respond with a barrage of more swear words, and she'd just throw her eyes to heaven.

But behind all the harum-scarum he was very kind and soft and had the best heart in the world.

Seamas gathered people like stray animals. After he began serving his time as a chef, he'd frequently arrive home with work colleagues. Some were people from other countries and he'd take them to our house for their tea.

As soon as he was able to afford it, Seamas bought himself an old scooter that would constantly break down or run out of petrol. He was a mad soccer fan and played with a local team. Every Sunday he'd head off to a match at different parks around Dublin city, sometimes taking me on the back of the scooter with him. Although my mother kept tight reins on me, I was allowed to go off on those Sunday morning adventures with Seamas.

He really was the golden boy in her world.

Brian was a lot more reserved and way better behaved than our Seamas, but he was a good character too. He was a very handsome young man with dark curly hair. Brian eventually gave up on Irish dancing before he achieved his full potential.

By then, of course, I had taken over the baton, after getting into a dancing class through him. Brian's passion was also cooking and he got a scholarship to the Coláiste Mhuire Cookery School in Dublin's Cathal Brugha Street. Later he worked in Dublin's very exclusive Shelbourne Hotel on St Stephen's Green as a chef. Then he moved to Mullingar, Co. Westmeath, where he opened up his own restaurant in the midland town.

When my last brothers left home in their late teens, one after the other, I finally had a bedroom of my own and was no longer forced to share my parents' room. This was bittersweet, because while I was excited to have a room all to myself, there was the sadness and loneliness of not having my brothers around. I really missed their voices around the house, and the interaction I had with them. But I guess every family has to come to terms with that empty nest syndrome, as it's called in today's world.

I sensed that my mother was lonely without them too, but at least she still had me. And when I think back to those early days in my life, I see how much effort she put into giving me the opportunities to grow into an educated young woman with some good social skills and talents.

Along with the Irish dancing classes, my mum somehow found the money to continue funding my music tuition. I have no doubt that she deprived herself of little treats in order to be in a position to give me those opportunities to become accomplished at music and dancing.

However, my young life felt like a constant struggle because of my chronic lack of confidence around people. I remember one time Seamas brought me into the restaurant in Pims Department Store in South Great George's street in the city. Seamas put me sitting at a table and then he went off and returned with an ice cream. But I couldn't eat it because I felt that all of the people in the restaurant were looking at me.

I was so introverted, and I still think that was the result of not being allowed to mix on our street with the other children during very important years of development as a young child.

I eventually gave up music after my mother changed me from Johnny Fox's classes and enrolled me at the College of Music in Dublin's Chatham Street, where I discovered that I was a child in an adult class. It also meant a bus journey into town. I stuck with it for a few years, but unlike the dancing I never felt comfortable doing the music.

When I first started off in Chatham Street the music lessons were private and on a one-to-one basis. But when I went to a theory class I'd find myself with other people and I would always be really self-conscious and a bag of nerves when I had to do the scale exercises and sing them out loud.

The reason I was in with older people is that I was actually doing quite well in music and had moved up to higher grades. But my stomach would churn as I waited my turn to stand up and give my little performance. I knew even then that one thing I would never be able to do is sing.

I also knew that I could never do a job like Aunt Em's.

MY ADVENTURES

WITH AUNT EM

Aunt Em moved from Artane to our side of the city after she was appointed district midwife in the Crumlin area. She then bought what I considered to be a posh house on Sundrive Road.

Her beautiful new family abode, with its lovely big rooms all tastefully decorated, was within walking distance of our home, and my mother would regularly send me over there on little errands.

This led to me getting quite close to Aunt Em.

I don't know how it all began, but somewhere along the line I became her travelling companion whenever she was called out to deliver a baby. As a twelve-year-old child, this was quite an ordeal for me and an experience I would never forget.

The drama would start before we left the driveway of Aunt Em's lovely home.

She had just taken up driving and had bought herself a little second-hand black Morris Minor car. But, as gutsy and stoical as she was in every other aspect of life, driving seemed to terrify the life out of her.

Sometimes we would sit in the Morris Minor for half and hour while Aunt Em sat sighing, fidgeting and fretting as she plucked up the courage to turn the key in the ignition.

Eventually, after several false starts, the car would bounce out on to the road like it had just been caught in some kind of whirlwind. After the unfortunate little vehicle roared into life, more often than not there would be terrible grinding noises as Aunt Em crudely stuck it into gear.

Finally, we'd hop along in mad spurts, with the engine often cutting out. Then she'd give it another go, putting the poor car through more torture. I'd glance over at Aunt Em from the corner of my eye and see her staring wildly ahead, her face as white as a sheet as we finally took off.

Here I have to spare a thought for all the women in labour who were anxiously awaiting the arrival of this midwife in those times, because Aunt Em certainly wasn't the rapid response unit. The Morris Minor would crawl along the quiet city streets at four or five miles an hour, chugging and spluttering and often cutting out.

She really had no idea how to drive and probably shouldn't have been out on the road. It was an endurance test for the two of us. I often wondered why I had to be there, but I guess she needed the company to get through her obvious fear of driving.

Sitting beside me in the car, in a stiff, straight position and with her face pressed against the windscreen, Aunt Em looked every inch the district nurse. She was dressed in her impeccable white uniform with a navy gaberdine over it. She wore a little round hat down to her eyebrows, and her slightly stern look was completed with glasses that sat on the bridge of her nose.

Lying on the backseat of the Morris Minor was her little black medical satchel, the contents of which were a wonder to me.

If I was one of her clients and I spotted Aunt Em coming through my bedroom door I think I'd be so terrified by the look of her I would give birth on the spot. Yet I heard so many stories throughout my life of her kindness to the young mothers, and how she would make return visits carrying gifts of food and clothes where she felt the need arose.

Although her blood pressure would be sky-high by the time we reached our destination, Aunt Em always seemed to quickly recover her composure as she slipped into her role as a midwife.

Sometimes I'd sit in the car, often for hours, while I patiently waited for the arrival of a new baby into the world. On many other occasions I'd be put sitting in the parlour of homes, watching basins of hot water going up and down stairs. I'd shudder as I heard the cries of women in the throes of labour.

That strange experience certainly put the fear of God into me about having children. When I'd eventually hear the cry of a baby I'd know that whatever was going on upstairs in the bedroom was nearly over and I'd soon be going home.

The return journey was another adventure with a very stressed-out Aunt Em, as she once again grappled with the challenge of controlling her car.

I don't know how we got around the streets of our Dublin suburb without causing some dreadful damage to an unfortunate human or object, but by sheer luck or divine intervention Aunt Em never had an accident. It probably helped that there were very few cars on the road at the time, and that she drove at a snail's pace.

Strange as it may seem, I never had a conversation with Aunt Em about babies, despite all the time we were together before and after she carried out her role as a midwife. What went on in the rooms of the houses that I spent long hours in as Aunt Em brought a new human being into the world wasn't spoken of. She never educated me on how babies were conceived, what pregnancy was all about, or how a child was born.

Aunt Em never brought it up, and I never asked her, because that's just the way it was in those times. It was left to my imagination – and that wasn't a good thing. All I could think about was the roars of women crying out in pain upstairs in the rooms where Aunt Em went to work.

And I knew then that I was never, ever going to be a midwife.

* * *

The humiliation of being held back a year in primary school continued to be my motivation for learning and increased my dedication towards school and then college. After my education in Terenure, I went on to the College of Commerce in Rathmines. I was one hundred per cent focused on studying, and I was like a sponge soaking up everything that I was being taught.

My target was to be in the top three of whatever subject we were doing in college. My mother recognised my passion for education and she was supporting me financially, having got a job with St James's Hospital as an ambulance assistant to bring in an income as my father was now too ill to work. When they went out on emergency calls, she would be the assistant in the ambulance.

My poor father's health was rapidly deteriorating and he really didn't have much quality of life. There were periods when he would be seriously ill and very weak, and he was constantly in and out of hospital.

Watching my lovely father struggling with even minor tasks tore at my heart. Finally, at his lowest point, Dad was admitted to St James's Hospital where my mother was working.

A week later he passed away peacefully.

I was just sixteen years old. Although I was heartbroken, as all of us were in the family, there was some consolation in the knowledge that Dad was now at peace and free of pain.

* * *

When I got my diploma after three years in the College of Commerce, I went for an interview for a job in the bank, where they told me that I was too young and to come back in a year. I wasn't at all disappointed as I didn't feel ready to go into the workplace. I was hungry to learn more.

So next I got a place in Caffrey's Secretarial College, a commercial college on St Stephen's Green in the city. I was now becoming a professional academic with the financial backing of my mother, who had continued working in St James's after Dad died, but was now stationed in the admissions unit.

I was only a couple of months in Caffrey's when they asked me to help out in their college office. They told me that as I clearly knew most of the course which I was studying, I could do some practical work instead.

Essentially they then employed me as an unpaid office worker.

When my mother discovered that I was working in the college she hit the roof.

'What's going on here?' she asked angrily. 'I'm paying for you to go to college and you're working in their office for nothing!'

When I told the college about my mother's objections they immediately put me back on the course.

I always recognised and appreciated the support I was getting from my mother, and the personal sacrifices she made to educate me.

After my father died, the only treat she would allow herself was a Friday night out at the bingo in Sundrive. On one of those Friday nights Mum came home beaming from ear to ear. She had won the jackpot and picked up one hundred pounds, which was a small fortune at the time.

At this point, my Aunt Em had emigrated to America with her son, Tom. They went over to New York in November 1963, the same month that President John F. Kennedy was shot dead in Dallas.

Aunt Em left Ireland with Tom, who was then in his early twenties, because she felt he would find better opportunities in life over there. I remember begging Aunt Em to take me too. I was then eighteen and I too wanted to get out of Ireland and try a different life.

This was too much responsibility for Aunt Em at the time and I was so disappointed when she turned me down. However, she explained that she wanted to get settled there first, and then I could follow her.

After Aunt Em left I knew that my mother had a desire to visit her in New York, and I insisted that the money she won hitting the jackpot in bingo that night should be set aside for the trip.

So that's what Mum did. She headed off on her dream trip to the States while I went to stay with Matt Meleady, his wife Angela and their young children at their home in Glasnevin.

The Meleadys had become like a second family to me. I often stayed with them, babysitting and helping with the housework. And I grew very close to their eight children: Aoibheann, Feargal, twins Eimir and Doireann, Colm, Niall (my godson), and twins Eoin and Maitiu.

They were like younger brothers and sisters to me and I helped their mother, Angela, to raise them and look after them. I used to take them to school, and to their dancing classes. Angela was a typical Irish mother who was very homely, always cooking meals, and totally devoted to the needs of her children.

* * *

Outside of college, Irish dancing was the major passion in my life. From about the age of twelve, my head was constantly spinning with ideas for creating steps and movement.

I choreographed my first Irish dance steps at that age. In those days we used to say, 'I made up a step.' The word 'choreography' didn't come into the vocabulary until years later. So I was making up steps, inventing my own dances, and I loved it. I lived for it.

When I became a teenager, it was time to move from the Inis Ealga dancing class and join the seniors in Craobh an Chéitinnigh, the Keating branch of the Gaelic League.

I also did some drama there, working alongside people like Martin Dempsey, who would go on to become a famous Irish actor.

Every Sunday during my early days I'd be dancing in competition at some feis, accompanied by my mum. As we didn't have a car, we hopped on buses or took a train to places like Skerries and Drogheda.

At the feis I'd dance on the small flat trailer of a lorry or tractor in the open air. The little trailer would accommodate a judge sitting at a table, a musician and three dancers. How we ever managed to perform without tripping and flying over the edge I'll never know. There certainly was no such thing as health and safety in those times.

My mother was forever scrimping and saving to make sure that I kept up my dancing. There was a lot of expense, particularly as we often travelled abroad to take part in festivals. My first trip was at the age of thirteen; we went to Germany, where we did an exchange and stayed with local families.

There was also a great festival in the Isle of Man in those times and we took part in that for many years. So from a very young age, Irish dancing was my passport to the world outside our little island of Ireland and my sheltered existence in Dublin.

I never dreamt just how far it would take me as my life unfolded.

But as my college days drew to an end, I was now getting deeper and deeper into the world of Irish dancing, and starting out on the road to becoming a professional teacher myself.

A DANCE TEACHER

IS BORN

I was eighteen when I danced in competition for the last time, and the trauma of that day created the teacher and trainer that I became in life.

The year was 1963 and I was taking part in the All-Ireland Irish Dancing Championships in the magnificent old Mansion House, the official home of the Lord Mayor of Dublin and a near-perfect venue for lots of prestigious events.

As I awaited my turn to dance, nerves were slowly creeping up and getting a grip on me like a devil in the night. I couldn't fight them because, quite frankly, in that moment I didn't feel that I was an elite dancer.

Our school was good, but we weren't one of the top dancing classes in the country at that time. I knew that the exceptional Irish dancing classes in that era were run by Cora Cadwell, Ita Cadwell and Harry McCaffrey. They were the top guns of the day.

Out of loyalty I had stuck with my own class and now here I was participating in the All-Ireland Championships with the awful feeling that I wasn't going to measure up.

I had won senior championships along the way because I worked by myself as I got older. But I was yet to win an All-Ireland competition. This was the first time I had a decent chance and I was buckling under with pressure as I knew the standard was exceptionally high.

By the time I stepped up on stage to dance, I was literally trembling.

As I waited for the music to start the energy drained from my body and I could feel my right knee shaking like it had a life of its own. And what flashed through my mind in that moment was the thought: 'When I become a teacher I am going to train and drill my class so well that none of them will ever feel nerves like this on stage.'

* * *

Every day after Caffrey's commercial college, I'd take the bus and go straight to Matt's dance class. At this stage I was helping him to teach dancing and I was doing all the choreography. It wasn't a paid job; I was doing it for the love of it. Outside of school and then college, dancing became a world that I was totally immersed in.

When I finished my course in Caffrey's, it was Matt who got me my first job as a secretary. I went to work for the affable Dermot Doolan, who was general secretary of Irish Actors Equity at the time. I became Dermot's personal secretary and we were running the casting for extras in films.

After work I would then go straight to dance class, spending every spare hour there. Even though I enjoyed my job, I was always looking forward to dancing. I began to think about it as a career in life.

How good it would be to make a living doing something that you loved so much!

Two years into my Actors Equity secretarial job I took the plunge to become a full-time Irish dancing teacher.

My working life as a dance teacher began in the national (primary) schools of Dublin, starting off at Mother of Divine Grace in Finglas and Holy Faith Convent in Glasnevin, then branching out from there.

Each day of the week I'd go into a different school and teach students from first class up to sixth, doing twenty minutes with each of the groups of young people. The principal of the school would pay me an hourly rate.

I taught up to 400 students in a school every day, and then that evening I'd go to Matt's and teach there on a voluntary basis. Every day was full-on, teaching from nine in the morning until eleven at night. This left no time for me to have a social life or friends my own age to hang out with. But I would often think to myself at that point in my life, well, it doesn't really matter because you love what you're doing.

And I did.

So I continued to work all the hours that God sent me.

* * *

My mother returned home from America and she couldn't stop herself singing the praises of that land of opportunity. Mum had had a great time in New

York with Aunt Em, who took her under her wing and helped her heal after the loss of my father.

As we talked for endless hours about her experiences in the States, my mother would stress how she felt there was a good life waiting for me there if I was interested in taking the leap, adding that she would emigrate with me. She was planting a seed, because by now my initial dream of a life in New York was no longer driving me.

I think my mother, being wise and intuitive, saw that dancing had consumed my young world to the detriment of every other aspect of life. She could probably see that I needed to break away in order to get a perspective on where I was going with my life.

I told her I would think about it, that maybe I could work there teaching Irish dancing.

However, it would be a while before I could consider that as I needed to do my teacher's exam and get my certificate when I turned twenty-one, which was the required age.

As my work continued in the national schools, I branched into shows not thinking for one moment that this would prove to be great experience for me in the years ahead. I had no dreams of being in show business at that point in my life. It really just happened in a very natural way.

Every year the schools would put on an end-of-year dance display, or drill displays as they called it, for the parents before the summer break in May or June. When I first started doing this, I realised that it was actually quite boring for the parents to have to sit through class after class coming out and doing Irish dance after Irish dance. I felt some variety could be introduced to break it up … and that's how the shows began.

Every year I would then produce a different musical, such as *Oliver!*, *Fiddler on the Roof* or *Joseph and the Amazing Technicolour Dreamcoat,* with the cast made up mostly of sixth-class pupils.

Some of the schools, like Marino, had huge numbers and their own drama teachers, so we shared the work. The talent that emerged every year was just incredible. We saw little stars born year after year. The classes that weren't involved in the musicals provided the entertainment with their Irish dancing displays, and I also choreographed dance routines for different songs in the show. So that's where I got my first experience of staging big shows.

At that time there was a variety talent contest in Ireland called Tops of the Town, and the teachers in the schools would say of our productions: 'These are every bit as good as the Tops of the Town.'

The show became the highlight of every school year. I was obsessed with it and every spare hour at home was spent on show preparation, working on the costumes and the production. The teachers loved it too and they all got involved, making costumes and doing various bits and pieces.

Sister Mary, the principal in Marino, was enthusiastically supportive of what we were producing every year, and she gave me the run of the whole school to prepare a new show.

She'd tell her teachers, 'Whatever class Marie wants for as long as she wants goes to the hall for rehearsals.'

The shows became so big and so good and so professional that everyone, from the school principals to the teachers and students, were immensely proud of their involvement and got such a great kick out of it.

* * *

I passed the T.C.R.G. examination and became a certified Irish dance teacher in my twentieth year, which meant I could now enter my pupils in competitions.

By this stage the Inis Ealga name was building and building, and Matt asked me to continue with him as a voluntary teacher. I agreed, but started my own classes on Mondays and Thursdays because Matt didn't have Inis Ealga classes on those days.

My classes were still under the banner of Inis Ealga, but they became known as 'Marie's class'. I still attended and taught the other classes for free, but the Monday and Thursday fees were for myself.

From the outset, I had a clear vision of what I wanted to do with my young dancers. My ambition was not just to make a champion, but for everyone in my classes to be as good as one another.

And that went back to the moment I stood on stage at the All-Ireland Championships with my knee shaking.

I wanted my pupils to be so well trained and so self-assured as regards their ability and skill that they would step out on any stage full of confidence. That's why I didn't concentrate on picking individual champions from my classes. I made sure that every individual dancer got the same attention, the same coaching, and were as good as each other.

Years down the line I was asked, 'How did you produce so many Irish dancing champions?'

That's how I did it.

* * *

All the new kids who came into Inis Ealga were joining the Monday and Thursday class to build it up. Soon we were entering competitions from beginner's stage, and doing exceptionally well. I began to build a little bit of a reputation as people started to take note of the success rate that my batch of dancers were achieving, and applications for membership of my classes began to mount up.

However, it was all work and no play, as they say, and eventually I started to question where I was going with my life. As much as I loved the Meleady family and Inis Ealga, I wanted the freedom to do other things.

But as Inis Ealga grew into an empire and invitations stacked up for us to do workshops worldwide, this became more and more impossible. I didn't know how long I could continue living with that kind of pressure and the restrictions it imposed on my personal life.

Not that I had a personal life.

There had been some brief romances, but none of the guys hung around. It didn't help that there were always three of us in the relationship: the boyfriend, myself … and Irish dancing.

By contrast, my childhood friend Beryl had the perfect balance in her life. Beryl had a job working in a major department store on South Great George's Street as an assistant. One morning on her way to work Cupid obviously contrived to link up Beryl with the man of her dreams – at her local bus stop.

Ciaran, the lovely guy she went on to marry, was working nearby and they struck up a conversation and hit it off.

Love blossomed and grew, and when Beryl and Ciaran got married, I was among the guests invited to celebrate their special day. It was a beautiful wedding for a really lovely couple.

In a way, Beryl was like a sister to me. We had both been little girls playing together in our homes on Cashel Road in Crumlin, and staring out the window at the boys having so much fun on the street.

Those childhood memories always stay with you.

I was delighted to hear the news when Beryl became a mum for the first time, and that more children filled her and Ciaran's world. Beryl and Ciaran were two great people who bring back fond memories to me. However, with the passing of time our lives went in different directions and we eventually lost touch.

But like all close friends, if we met in the morning we'd just pick up where we left off.

THE ROLO KID

'Look, it's the Rolo kid!'

The words rang out in my ears as I passed people on the street.

Strangers were pointing and shouting in my direction.

I was mortified, but secretly a little bit chuffed as well.

For a few years in the early 1960s I was a little bit famous. Not as a dancer. Not as a teacher. But, strange as it may seem, for a 'my last Rolo' advertisement on Telefís Éireann!

In the TV advert for the chocolate-covered toffee sweets that was broadcast nightly, I was one of three Irish dancers acting out a scene based around the storyline of 'my last Rolo'.

We were dressed in the old-fashioned Irish dancing costume with a cloak on the back, and there was a pocket stitched on to the one that I was wearing.

I had a dancer each side of me, we did a couple of steps and at the end of it I reached into the pocket on my costume and produced a packet of Rolos. I shared them with the other dancers, and then there was one left for me.

The advert ended with the camera focused on my face as I chewed my last Rolo, desperately trying to convey with scrunched-up facial expressions how delicious it tasted. Not a good look!

I have a friend, James, who says he won't rest until he finds a copy of that Rolo advert and sticks it up on YouTube to embarrass me today.

* * *

The magic of television had arrived into Ireland in December 1962 with the launch of Telefís Éireann, and the following year I made my first appearance on an Irish music and dance show called *Beirt Eile*, which was co-hosted by Liam Devally and Kathleen Watkins. Liam was a very popular Irish personality and singer who went on to become a barrister and then a top court judge. Kathleen Watkins later married Gay Byrne, one of Ireland's greatest ever broadcasters who made his mark as the host of *The Late Late Show* on television.

Telefís Éireann had signed up Matt, or Maitiu Ó Maoiléidigh as he was known, to organise the music and dancing content of *Beirt Eile*. The senior dancers on the show were from Inis Ealga, and that is where I first started on television, doing céilí dancing as part of a group of dancers. We'd do the two-hand, the four-hand, the eight-hand, all the different céilí dances, and that would be interspersed with the céilí bands, solo musicians and singers. And once a month Matt would run the céilí practice for the TV one night during the week, and then we'd record two programmes on the same day, with the show being aired on a Friday night.

Beirt Eile ran for two years, and then it was replaced with a new TV show called *Club Céilí*, a bilingual programme of Irish music, song and dance. The host, or Feár An Tí as he was called, was Sean Duignan, a strikingly hand-some young man who went on to work with RTÉ news and as a political correspondent for forty years. Sean also served as press secretary to the Fianna Fáil–Labour Party government in the early 1990s.

Matt too had a central role on the show, as well as being the content organiser. Matt had a gregarious, outgoing personality and a great sense of humour with a quick smile. He really shone in situations like that. The camera, as they say, loved him, so he looked good on screen. And he had the likeability factor, which is an essential ingredient for the success of any personality, no matter how talented they are.

One of the features of *Club Céilí* was a dance class in which Matt created a new céilí dance for two, four or eight people. He would showcase a different dance every week. And once a month the Inis Ealga group would do a special performance or solo dance in which I constantly appeared.

Matt always had great foresight and a brilliant mind for creating choreography. I was given a high-profile role in this segment of the show because I was the dancer who demonstrated the new steps. This was no easy task as I had to do the moves in slow motion while maintaining my balance – all the while keeping a big smile on my face. Then a group of us would do the lessons and the dances.

While Inis Ealga became the resident dancers on *Club Céilí*, Matt also opened it up to other dance classes from around the country. In that period I made some lifelong friends with dancers who appeared on the show, including Seamus and Aine O'Shea and Noreen Flanagan Duggan, who are well known in the Irish dancing world as they went on to become C.L.R.G. teachers and adjudicators and members of An Coimisiún, the governing body of Irish dance.

The two TV shows ran over four years in total, so the exposure we got in Ireland was tremendous. They were Friday night shows and that was prime-time television, particularly as there was no competition from other stations at the time. To have a Friday night slot was huge.

I couldn't help but notice the recognition it gave me at the time due to the fact that I was a regular feature on every show, doing specialised performance pieces, or a solo dance, in front of the camera.

As we were in one-channel-TV land at the time, there was no escaping me.

What I really loved about doing those television shows is the fact that it made my mother so proud. There was her daughter *Mar*-ee on the telly, with all the neighbours on the street, or at least those who had televisions, watching her perform. So all Mum's struggles to get me to do music and dancing in hard financial times had now paid off. I could see that she was really chuffed, even though I don't imagine she ever expected me to be on television. But there I was: *Mar*-ee Duffy the TV dance star and Rolo ad celebrity.

* * *

I spent several years working on Telefís Éireann with Matt in the 1960s. Matt was the go-to person whenever they needed dancers for shows, so we organised them.

Seamus Ennis, the celebrated Irish uileann piper, singer and Irish music collector, had worked for the BBC in London and when he returned to Ireland Telefís Éireann gave him a Saturday morning children's programme. Matt was once again asked to provide the children for that show, and I worked on it with him.

I loved the challenge of that show because it wasn't straightforward children's dancing. We also had to create different games for the young people to play on the TV. So we invented street games with footballs and ropes and things like that. We even gave hopscotch a new twist.

I did that show every Saturday morning and looking back today I realise how great it was to be involved in the early days of Irish television. And, without being aware of it, I was learning new skills that would benefit me, and the people I worked with, in my later career.

With his flair for creating new styles of choreography, Matt took Inis Ealga into the hotels where we started doing exhibitions at their cabaret shows. This was in the early stages of Irish dancing being tweaked to become show dancing.

When two Irish showbiz personalities, Eamon Andrews and Fred O'Donovan, launched Jury's Cabaret, they hired us as the dancers. Irish comedian Hal Roache was the star of that show, which became a major attraction for Irish-American tourists and ran for several decades. In fact, it went into the Guinness Book of Records as the longest running cabaret show in Ireland.

* * *

My mother went back to America, where she was living with Aunt Em in Rockaway Beach, Queens, New York, thinking that I would follow her out. She was really keen on me making the break from Inis Ealga because she felt it would be for my own good. Although I was now working at a very high level, it was relentless. There was no sign of me settling down with a man – trying to hang on to one was like catching a wet bar of soap – and I think she felt it was something I would come to regret later in life. She could see time running out for me. But I couldn't make the break at the time.

'Well, if you're not coming out I'm going home,' Mum told me in an exasperated tone on the phone one day.

And so she did. Back to our house on Cashel Road.

The next time Mother returned to New York it was to look after Aunt Em, as her health was then deteriorating. She was hospitalised and suffering from very bad emphysema. Mum went over to spend time with her, and to ensure that she had all the support she needed in her final days on earth. She stayed with my cousin, Tom, and his wife, Arline, and would go to the hospital a couple of times a day.

I was very upset when Aunt Em passed away in July 1971. Even though it was a happy release for her, as emphysema is a terrible lung disease, it was still heartbreaking to be told that she was gone.

Aunt Em had been quite a character. Even to this day, whenever we get together as a family the stories about that remarkable woman are always a great source of amusement.

I remember that one time she came home on a visit after her first year in America and we all noticed that she looked years younger.

'Where have all her wrinkles gone?' my brother Brian laughed.

We couldn't stop staring at her.

All the wrinkles she left Ireland with had disappeared. They hadn't invented Botox in those days, but whatever potion she found over there had certainly worked. There wasn't a crease to be seen on her face.

Aunt Em's terrible driving skills and her motoring escapades have also provided us with endless amusement. A famous story told about her in the family is the day she drove out to the countryside to visit one of my uncle Martin's daughters. Aunt Em, of course, was notorious for torturing the gearboxes of cars. As she set off for home after her country visit that day the only gear she could engage was reverse. And so she drove all the way back to the city … in reverse!

As many people found to their cost, Aunt Em was not a woman to be messed with. My cousin, Tom, has a vivid memory of his mother confronting a sadistic teacher who had sent him home one afternoon with swollen hands after a particularly vicious caning in school when he was just seven years old.

The next morning Aunt Em accompanied Tom to the school. After all the young pupils had settled in to their classroom, she knocked on the door of Tom's teacher, smiled in his direction, and with a curled finger she invited him to join her in the hallway.

When the six-foot-two tall teacher stepped out of the classroom Aunt Em then produced a handgun and told the terrified monster that if he ever sent her son home in that condition again both she and the gun would return ... and this time she would shoot him with no questions asked.

At that moment the school principal arrived on the scene and interrupted her little 'discussion'. The principal immediately invited her to step into his office – at which point Tom's teacher took off up the hall like a scalded cat.

The principal said he had a good mind to call the guards and have her arrested for threatening the teacher with a gun.

Aunt Em told him to 'go right ahead'!

But there the matter ended.

The principal, it transpired, was an Old IRA member who had fought alongside her in the War of Independence. However, he did seek a promise from Aunt Em that she would never again bring a gun on to the school premises. And I doubt that it was ever called for again.

I had grown very close to Aunt Em during my early years and I really yearned to say goodbye to her when she died. So it was lovely that my cousin Tom took his mother's remains home to Ireland to be buried with her family, the O'Kellys, in Glasnevin Cemetery. It allowed us all to pay our final respects and to give her a good Irish send-off.

Aunt Em went out with a bang – literally. Having been an active soldier of Ireland, she was buried with full military honours, including the tapping of drums and a volley of shots fired over her graveside.

Tom went on to enjoy a very good life in America, fulfilling his mother's dream. It was there that he met his Irish-American wife, Arline, and the couple, who now live in North Carolina, started a family together and reared three fine sons, Thomas, Dennis and Frederick (Fritz).

When he first moved to America, Tom trained as a bartender and ran Hurley's bar and restaurant on the corner of New York's Radio City venue for many years. It was a very famous bar around theatre-land and lots of stars frequented it through the decades.

When I started doing Irish dancing workshops in America during the 1970s, I always made a point of dropping in to Hurley's to catch up with Tom and to reminisce about old times while also bringing him up to date on happenings in our family.

* * *

Come 1969 there was a war of sorts going on in the world of Irish dancing, with Matt in the middle of it.

The dance teachers set up their own organisation, known as An Comhdháil (The Congress of Irish Dance Teachers). Then they had a falling out with the governing body, An Coimisiún Le Rincí Gaelacha, or C.L.R.G. as it's known.

Some of the big schools in Dublin split with An Coimisiún at this point. And to build up the Coimisiún again, Matt and a number of other individuals came up with the idea of launching the Irish Dancing World Championships.

Their grand ambition of putting Irish dancing on the world stage was ridiculed at the time. Their critics scoffed at the idea, declaring that it was ludicrous to expect people to travel from places likes America and Australia.

'You're off your head,' they told him.

But, undaunted, Matt persevered and established the structure, which was like a pyramid. The bottom rung was the regional championships, and then you had the national championships and finally the world championships at the top.

Needless to say, I was sucked into more work. I became Matt's personal assistant for the running of this world event.

We started organising it from Matt's home, where all the entries would come in and I'd do the secretarial work. Cups and trophies had to be organised, and I recall one time Matt insisting that everyone who qualified should get some kind of recognition, so we had to go looking for sponsorship.

Fergal Quinn, one of Ireland's great entrepreneurs and the founder of Superquinn, was a good friend of Matt and he was very generous to us at that time.

And from humble beginnings in the tiny theatre of Coláiste Mhuire in Dublin's Parnell Square in 1969, the championships have grown into a huge international event.

The first World Championships were held over a weekend in Coláiste Mhuire; now it's an eight-day event, starting on the Sunday before Easter, and is worth over £10 million to the local economy of any city that hosts it, so it is well sought after worldwide. I'm still an active member of the committee for this event.

* * *

Not only were the World Championships a great success for Irish dancing, they also introduced me to my first serious boyfriend.

Like every fairy-tale love story, our eyes met across a crowded room. The room in Coláiste Mhuire was crowded because it was the World Championships, but somehow I had picked out this handsome young man. There was a friendly nod and we casually got chatting, with the conversation rolling easily as the common topic was Irish dancing. I remember being taken with his lovely accent. John, I'll call him, was from London.

It's fair to say I was smitten fairly quickly, and the attraction was mutual. Amid all the organised chaos around us we talked like we'd known each other all our lives. Finally, we arranged to meet up when the day's schedule was over.

John had a genial personality and was a gentleman in the way he conducted himself. We spent a lovely time together and after the championships we kept in touch and continued to build on our relationship. The following year we attended the wedding of two dance teachers in Glasgow as a couple, and during that romantic occasion he proposed to me.

That summer John came over on holiday and he could see how busy my life was with Inis Ealga. We did get to spend time together and even went looking for rings, but we never made a decision on one. I don't know if that was a sign that maybe we were having second thoughts about how our lives would work together.

When John returned to Scotland after that holiday the relationship slowly fizzled out. It was an amicable parting and we kept in touch over the years. But for years afterwards, while I was still on my own, I would often wonder if John had cooled on the relationship because my life had been so absorbed with Inis Ealga. And if I hadn't been so caught up in my work there, would I have been more open to a life with him? Would we have married, set up home together and reared children?

It's not a conversation I ever had with him.

Whatever the reason, it was a love story without the fairy-tale ending.

INIS EALGA GOES GLOBAL

I had no idea that Irish dancing would open doors that would lead me to an international career of sorts.

Pop and rock stars were jet-setting around the globe in those heady days of the sixties and seventies, criss-crossing the Atlantic and flying to exotic locations. It never crossed my mind that teaching Irish dancing would also be my ticket to world travel. Inis Ealga gave me that opportunity.

The World Championships put Inis Ealga on the map, particularly after we had a winner in every championship. After that our name and reputation spread like a gorse fire during a long, hot summer.

Then came a shower of requests for us to do workshops with schools in North America where an Irish dancing scene had been established by people like Peter Smith, May Butler, Cyril McEniff, Fidelma Davis and Anne O'Sullivan.

I can still remember the excitement of getting on a plane to Canada after our first invitation from May and Paddy Butler of the famous Butler Academy in Toronto. May, a lovely, warm, graceful lady, was a native of Dalkey in south county Dublin, and she was running a very successful school in Toronto at the time.

We had become great friends with the Butlers because we'd meet them when they came home on holiday to Dublin every year with their young children, June and Patrick.

At this point Inis Ealga had become quite famous for our figure choreography and dance drama. Our solo dancers were doing well in every age group. I had trained each dancer to the same standard, fulfilling a pledge I had made to myself when I'd struggled with my confidence the last time I'd danced competitively in the All-Ireland Championships.

Paddy Butler was impressed by our dancers and he made the approach to Matt at the championships.

'What would it take to get you guys out to Toronto?' Paddy asked. 'Would you come out and teach us that dance?'

So off we went, Matt and myself, for a month of teaching. The air trip was an adventure in itself. Firstly, we had to make our way to Scotland as the chartered flight to Toronto was from Prestwick. The glamour of jet-setting was stripped away shortly after we took off. The plane was packed to capacity, people were smoking all around me, and they ran out of food shortly after the in-flight service had started.

My childlike excitement quickly abated.

This felt like a trip from hell.

By the time we landed in Toronto, I felt like we'd gone around the world in eighty days. I was so glad to be stepping off that plane, but my excitement levels were soon back up when Paddy and May arrived to whisk us off to our base in the city. They were the perfect hosts: warm, welcoming and full of fun.

Our assignment in Toronto was like a secret service mission, an undercover job. May and Paddy didn't want other local teachers to know that we had been hired in as specialists to teach a particular dance.

I had developed my own methods of specific training, with warm-up exercises and drilling that had never been done before. This was a novelty for the dancers at the Butler school and they embraced it all. I couldn't have asked for more enthusiastic students. They willingly opened up to my tuition and absorbed my dancing tips. Many of them would go on to make their mark winning major titles.

I am proud to say that from my very first workshop, and the others that followed over the following couple of years, some very successful teachers, including Rosie Fearon and Yvonne Kelly, to name but two, emerged. They became world-class teachers who produced world champions themselves.

At the end of that month, during which Paddy and May took us to see the sights and were very generous with their hospitality, it was time to step on to another flight from hell. This time the return journey across the Atlantic was worse because I knew what lay ahead. To add to the endurance test there were a lot of drunk people around me, and everyone was annoyed when the food ran out (again!).

My jet-setting life failed miserably to live up to my expectations. I'm sure it was all so different for Mick Jagger and Paul McCartney at the time.

We left Toronto with our secret mission still under wraps. Nobody twigged that the Butler school had drafted in some outside expertise.

A few months later, May and Paddy took one of their students to dance in

New York. Two friends of mine, Peter Smith and Cyril McNiffe, were at the competition and standing at the shoulders of May and Paddy as their dancer went through her routine.

'That dance looks very familiar,' Peter remarked mischievously.

'It looks very familiar to me too,' Cyril agreed.

'Indeed, it's very similar to something I've seen in Ireland,' Peter added with a knowing look.

May and Paddy refused to take the bait.

They admitted to nothing.

* * *

Inis Ealga dancers swept the boards at the World Championships every year over the next couple of decades, and my jet-setting career continued to flourish. I'm joking, of course, about the jet-setting. But every summer I would fly out to America to run workshops, give masterclasses and adjudicate at competitions. I worked long hours every day, but I earned really good money. This was lucrative work for something I loved doing, and now it was on an international scale.

While in America during those summers, I would think back on the conversations I had with my mother years earlier when she told me about the opportunities that were available to me in that part of the world. I realised that she was so right. With the contacts I had established through Irish dancing, I knew I could pick up a job at the drop of a hat in the US. And the more I became familiar with the States, the more I felt I could live there. Then work would take over and the moment would pass.

As always, I was so caught up with Inis Ealga that I didn't notice how life was passing me by at a terrifying speed. I was still on my own as well. There wasn't a sign of a man on the horizon, much to the dismay of my brother Seamas, who obviously felt I was wasting my life as a young woman.

'Will you for God's sake come back pregnant,' Seamas demanded one summer as I packed my bags for America.

I was absolutely shocked.

'Seamas I couldn't do that, think of the disgrace!' I told him, no doubt with the disgust showing on my face.

He argued it wasn't shameful at all.

'Where's the disgrace in that?' he asked.

Seamas was very broad-minded and wise in his ways. He didn't want me to lose out on motherhood just because I didn't have a partner.

'But who will I have a child with?' I asked.

'It doesn't matter who,' Seamas sighed, as if that wasn't important.

The argument continued. 'How could I rear a child on my own?'

'Betty and I will do it with you,' Seamas offered, referring to my lovely sister-in-law.

Seamas was ahead of his time, whereas I was way too conservative to contemplate something like that.

'I don't think Mother would take too kindly to me getting pregnant with no man in my life,' was my final word on the matter.

Seamas shook his head in frustration, accepting that he had lost the argument.

'I just hope it's not something you'll regret down the line,' he told me.

Seamas and his wife Betty had two fabulous children, Declan and Debbie, whom they had adopted. They were a very happy little family, and Debbie and Declan adored the ground that Seamas and Betty walked on. I believe that having found such immense happiness in his own life through children, Seamas didn't want me waking up one day regretting that I had squandered my chance of experiencing the gift of parenthood.

He was so in tune with the important things in life.

* * *

As my work involved travel, I did get the opportunity to meet lots of interesting males from different parts of the world through music and dancing. One of those was a guy from Czechoslovakia that I first encountered at a cultural event in the Isle of Man. Despite coming from different backgrounds and countries, we hit it off.

He was a musician with a Czechoslovakian group, spoke seven languages, was very intellectual and we were the same age. He was tall and slim with fair hair and he had a personality that was very gentle and quiet. He was a lovely man, but deep down I knew the relationship was doomed from the time it began, mainly due to the fact that we were living in different countries.

Because of the Communist regime in Czechoslovakia at the time, his travel was restricted, so I had to fly out to visit him. When I went there I wasn't blinded by passion or love, so I was sensible enough to realise that I could never settle where he lived. I told him as much because I didn't want to lead him on and give him false hope.

The relationship cooled, and eventually died away. But every now and then he would get in contact and we'd talk. Then I would go out to see him. This sort of carry-on continued over a few years, even though I couldn't see it going anywhere.

Eventually he wrote to my mother and pleaded with her to persuade me to move to Czechoslovakia to be with him.

Mother showed me the letter and asked my advice on what she should say in reply. I told her to ignore it. Judging by her expression, I think she felt I had made the right decision in this case.

So that was the end of the relationship.

He did contact me a few years later to say that he had got married and was the father of a young daughter. And he was surprised to learn that I was still a single woman.

* * *

My thirties came and went like a flash of lightning. Matt by now had made me a director of Inis Ealga to entice me to stay after I'd indicated that I was leaving at one point. Apart from lots of world champions that I had produced, I had nothing else to show for the previous two decades. As strange as this seems now, I was still living between the Meleady home and my mother's house. It wasn't until I turned forty that I finally had a wake-up call. I decided, man or no man, it was time for me to become totally independent, buy myself a house and put down some roots.

I felt I had left it far too late to move to America. I remember discussing it with Matt's wife, Angela, one day. I told her of my regrets at not moving to the States.

'You can still go,' Angela said.

'At this point I'm not going to leave my mother on her own,' I replied.

Mum was much older now and it was too late for her to emigrate and start a new life with me. I couldn't bring myself to leave without her.

One day I sat down with Mum and told her I was buying my own home on the north side of Dublin. Most of my work was on that side of the city. By my mother's expression you'd think I'd just told her that I was emigrating to Timbuktu.

'I want you to come with me,' I added, and her face lit up.

At this stage we owned our 1930s family home on Cashel Road in Crumlin, having bought it off Dublin Corporation. We discussed selling Cashel Road, and that was agreed. So, now I had some new excitement in my life, going on the hunt for my first house.

Over the following months, I'd cruise around the north-side suburbs in my little second-hand blue Austin car with my mother in the passenger seat, searching for my dream home. It was like a new hobby.

Even though I was born on the south side, I always had a hankering to live on the north side. My uncle Christie, who had a very successful upholstery business, lived in a gorgeous house facing the sea just outside the fishing village of Howth. And I remember trips there as a child.

When I was young we'd often go on family outings to Howth, taking a tram out from the city centre. That was always a nice Sunday outing with my mum and dad, and whoever else was around.

I remember one particular excursion on a Sunday afternoon in the summertime when Tony and Seamas were home on holidays with their wives, Lena and Betty. Along with Brian and Mum and Dad, I took a trip by hired boat from the pier in Howth to the Ireland's Eye island. We brought picnic food with us and had a lovely, leisurely afternoon there in the sunshine. It was so lovely that we lost all sense of time.

In the evening time, we packed up our bits and pieces and went searching for the boat for the trip back to the village. To our horror, there was no boat by the shore. After waiting for what seemed like an eternity, we finally accepted that we'd missed the last one back. We were now resigned to sleeping under the stars for the night. Fortunately, it was summer time, but the thought of sleeping in the open where God knows what kind of creepy-crawlies were going to be on the prowl in the dark terrified me.

Then Brian spotted a shape in the distance. As it came closer, whoops of joy went up from the lads. It was a boat!

'This is your lucky night,' the boat man laughed when he pulled up on to the island.

'I decided to make one more trip out to the island in case anyone had been left stranded.'

The house-hunting would continue until one day, while driving through Kinsealy, my search came to an end.

I WANT TO BREAK FREE

Relaxing in the front room of my lovely, cosy bungalow home on a leafy road in Kinsealy, I finally took stock of my life.

As I strolled down memory lane in my mind, with the sunshine streaming through the window, I acknowledged that Inis Ealga had been a rewarding adventure in so many ways, not least because of the wonderful friendships and close friends around the world it had introduced to my life. Then there were all the children I had trained, the young people I adored.

But here I was, a middle-aged woman just having bought her first home, unmarried, childless and still tied to a relentless schedule at the Inis Ealga school.

It had been a struggle in my mind for so long, but in that moment I resolved to take the next major step. I was going to leave Inis Ealga.

* * *

In a way I had become a victim of the phenomenal success of Inis Ealga at home and abroad. It became a giant in the world of Irish dancing, which meant I was now running a major operation that occupied my every waking hour of the day to the exclusion of virtually everything else. And I felt trapped there because I didn't want to let anyone down. So, in a way, I had made myself a prisoner within this popular school of dance.

In reality, there was nothing to stop me leaving at any time. But, out of a sense of loyalty to everyone, I never felt I could make the break. It took a lot of soul-searching, a lot of agonising, and even a lot of prayer in my favourite place of contemplation, Whitefriar Street Carmelite Church in the city, before I found the courage to move on.

It is hard to convey in words the terrible emotional trauma I experienced in the lead-up to my departure from Inis Ealga. I dreaded the moment when I would finally drop the bombshell that I was leaving. I had a queasy feeling in my stomach for weeks in the build-up to it. I had invested so much of my life in Inis Ealga, so leaving was going to be a very painful divorce for me. But I was also conscious that, to the children and parents, Marie Duffy and Inis Ealga were inseparable. I knew that I was going to cause devastation in a lot of people's lives when I left. But what could I do?

I thought long and hard about my exit, trying to find a way to leave without causing too much disruption in the school. I didn't want to damage the school in any way. I knew that if I set up a Marie Duffy school of dance, a lot of the parents would move their children with me. I felt that the only way to avoid this was to walk away from Irish dancing and embark on a new career in life.

Physical exercise has always been at the core of dancing for me. I always got my students to do warm-up exercises in order to avoid injuries when they were dancing on concrete and all sorts of floors. Every other form of dance, like ballet, were doing proper training and exercise, warming up and cooling down, and muscle toning. It bothered me that this wasn't applied to Irish dancing, where classes always started off cold, so I introduced it during my early days in Inis Ealga.

Later, the kids used to refer to my pre-dance routines as 'the Marie Duffy exercises'.

I always kept myself in shape by working out in a gym three times a week. So, when I was looking for a way out of Inis Ealga, it struck me that I could do gym work to earn a living. I then signed up for a diploma course at City Gym in Dublin, with a view to becoming an instructor. I was already familiar with all the gym equipment, and I knew that aerobics training would be easy to do. I could learn all about nutrition and become a nutritionist as well. This was all covered on the diploma course that I enrolled for, so now I had a plan in place and it was time to break the news.

* * *

In 1988, at the end of the All-Ireland Championships, I announced that I was leaving Inis Ealga. By then, Matt had an inkling that I was restless in my life. I think he had seen the writing on the wall for some time, but it was still a shock when I told him.

Even though I had prepared for this moment to ensure that it would cause the least disruption, it was like a death in the family. It was truly awful. There were kids crying, saying, 'You are leaving us, you are going away.' I was in bits, trembling and struggling to control my emotions. This was like walking away from my family because I had trained all those children from the time they could walk.

Then the parents were all around me, pleading with me to change my mind, asking if there was anything they could do to keep me there. I just shook my head. I was crying, and they could see that my decision to move on hadn't been taken lightly.

I woke up the following morning with a terrible feeling of depression, and a huge sense of loss. Inis Ealga was the first thing I would think about every morning. It was the first thing I thought about that morning, except that now it was no longer a part of my life. What followed was a period of mourning.

Although I still felt that I had made the right decision, it didn't stop my heart from being broken. Every evening when I left my course at the gym, I'd cry like a hungry child on the way to my car. I knew that just up the road the children I regarded as my own were in their dance class. I never expected to miss them this much. But I persevered, taking my new life a day at a time and trying not to dwell on the past.

The pain eased gradually and I could see the light coming into my life again. When I left Inis Ealga I held on to my classes in the national schools so that I'd have an income, and then in the evening I would do the course for the gym. There was one three-month period where I had to take time out of teaching for my course, but for most of the nine months I managed to juggle the two.

I was enjoying my diploma course, as I loved education and was passionate about it from the time I had been held back a year in primary school. Even during my Inis Ealga days I took a course at the Grafton Academy of dressmaking so that I could work on costumes for shows.

I also did a short course in a London school of hairdressing to style my pupils for their dance competitions. Back then, the dancers didn't wear wigs.

Some of the dancers would have great heads of hair; others would have poor hair. I took it seriously enough to learn how to style hair so that each child went out on stage happy with their appearance and feeling the same confidence.

So I was hungry for new skills and for more education all the time. I had even done a three-year public speaking diploma course at The Adult Education Institute in Eccles Street, Dublin, to overcome my nerves on the stage when I was faced with the task of doing stage management and announcements at the dancing competitions.

I was all about self-development, so whenever I had time on my hands I would fill it with one course or another.

My course in the gym covered the A to Z of everything from aerobics to weight training and nutrition, and when I graduated with my diploma I then had options for a new career path.

However, while I was prepared to leave Irish dancing, it seems Irish dancing wasn't ready to let me go. Several of the parents continued calling to my home in Kinsealy, pleading with me to reconsider my decision to give up teaching. I was flattered that they felt so strongly about what I had to offer their children.

Every time a parent came and talked with me, I would mull over the conversation afterwards. There was no way I was going back to Inis Ealga after finally taking the momentous decision in my life to cut the ties. But the parents who came to see me, or spoke to me by phone, weren't asking me to rejoin Inis Ealga. They wanted me to run my own classes for their children that I had been teaching before I left. They all stressed how much the children were missing me. Every time I talked to parents I felt guilt that I was denying their kids the skills I had as a teacher, and the great relationship I'd had with them.

After a while I began to get a proper perspective on my life. One of the people who helped me through it was my friend Laverne Showalter from Chicago. Laverne was like my big sister or a mother to me at that time, as she talked me through the huge emotional experience of cutting my ties with Inis Ealga.

I realised then that my love and passion for dancing hadn't diminished since I left Inis Ealga. I did feel that a weight had been lifted from my shoulders, but that was down to not having the burden of running the school. My life was simpler now, less demanding, and I had control over it. I began to think that maybe I could run an Irish dancing class, but on a smaller, more manageable scale.

In the end I relented and agreed that I would take on twelve of the children whose parents had become more like personal friends. I had one rule: I would not take on any Inis Ealga dancers who were current All-Ireland or world champions, nor would I take boys. If I took boys I felt that would split up the Inis Ealga teams – and they were renowned for the standard of their teams – and that wouldn't have been fair to the school. So that was agreed with the parents, although some of them were disappointed that I wasn't taking their sons, as I had been teaching them before I left.

And so I started with twelve pupils, including three O'Brien sisters, Derval, Niamh and Aoibheann. Their mother, Monica, had been among the parents who encouraged me to start teaching again for the championships.

I'm so glad I did.

Niamh and Aoibheann would go on to dance in the famous line at the 1994 Eurovision Song Contest. After *Riverdance*, they then joined *Feet of Flames* and *Lord of the Dance*.

And Niamh would later find true love in the world of dancing with her husband, Michael Flatley.

I first met the O'Brien girls while I was with Inis Ealga and also running a class once a week where they lived out in the country at Kilbride, Co. Meath. Their mother, Monica, had a great love of Irish music and dancing. Derval was just four when Monica took her to my class in Kilbride, and Niamh was soon on her heels as a three-year-old. Niamh would be running around the hall while Derval learned her one, two, threes. The youngest, Aoibheann, was in the pram at that stage, and she joined as soon as she was up on her feet.

Derval, Niamh and Aoibheann took to Irish dancing like ducks to water. As they developed and started showing real potential, Monica then asked me about taking them into the city classes at Inis Ealga in North Great George's Street. So they became regulars at Inis Ealga, and they went on to figure in the top three at competitions. Derval finished second on two occasions at the World Championships after being just narrowly pipped at the post. Emma Jane Lavin, who was world champion for many years, was in Niamh's class at the time. Niamh would always come second to Emma at major events. She was up there with the best of them.

Monica O'Brien then held a feis in Kilbride for quite a few years, so Derval, Niamh and Aoibheann were totally immersed in the world of Irish dancing as they were growing up.

* * *

As well as running the dancing classes, I didn't let my qualification as a gym instructor go to waste. I got some work in a local gym, but gradually the dancing took over full-time as my earnings grew.

The Marie Duffy School of Dancing opened in 1986 in Claude Hall, Drumcondra, where one of the parents had a connection. It had a wooden floor and a small stage, which was perfect for my needs. I had considered different names for my school. But my brother Seamas was there to steer me in the right direction.

'Why are you ashamed of your own name?' Seamas asked.

'I'm not!' I said indignantly.

'Well, The Marie Duffy School of Dancing it is then,' he declared.

The first test of The Marie Duffy School of Dancing came later that year at the World Championships, which were held in Cork. My winners over the previous couple of decades had been under the Inis Ealga flag. But now I was out on my own, flying my own flag, so it was my reputation as a dance teacher on the line. I was confident about my solo dancers, and they didn't disappoint. In fact, they performed beyond my expectations. When the results came in, I had three new world champions up on the podium, and none of my dancers finished lower than fourth or fifth place.

My biggest worry was the figure choreography category, because there were usually sixteen dancers in the group, and I only had fourteen. My other team was an eight-hand and they had been winners. I decided to have a go anyway to show people what I could do, and I organised the figure choreography in a style that would hide the missing members of the dance troupe.

I had never been so nervous in the build-up to a competition, not even when I was performing myself. I was so conscious of the fact that there were a lot of people, including everyone from Inis Ealga, waiting curiously to see what I was going to produce.

An eerie silence fell over the venue when the troupe came out on stage. I had never experienced anything like it. My heart was pounding as they performed, but I felt it went well.

Then there was the agonising wait for the results to come in. There were seven adjudicators, so it could go either way.

Finally the announcement came through, with the revelation that six of the judges had given us a first, making it a really convincing win. I was in tears, because this was a massive result for my school, a huge relief, and the start of a great new adventure.

* * *

A couple of weeks later, offers to do workshops in North America started arriving at my door. Some were from people and schools I had worked with through Inis Ealga, others were new.

I was thrilled.

This was an affirmation of my reputation in the world of Irish dancing. When I was with Inis Ealga, I'd often wonder if it was the school's reputation that had opened those doors for me in the States and Canada. To get schools across the Atlantic now sending me personal offers answered that question for me – and I'm the type of person who needs reassurance every now and then.

So my jet-setting career resumed with The Marie Duffy School. I loved the fact that those summer trips to America and Canada allowed me to experience life in other parts of the world.

'Man, this is living!' as the Americans would say.

That's how I felt about it. They were all-expenses-covered trips and I was paid a top rate by the hour. I lived with the people who ran the schools, which kept the expenses down and was much nicer than staying in hotels. It was so enjoyable, the families were great company and they all had lovely homes. And if I was doing a couple of workshops over the summer I'd split the air fares between the schools, which were located in different parts of America.

Peter Smith from New Jersey was one of the first people who invited me over to give workshops in his school. When I went over I could see straight away the main problem in his school: there was no order or discipline.

Lord rest him, Peter has now passed on, but the first night I arrived at his class I thought it was like New York's Grand Central Station. People were walking around, kids were dancing, parents were talking in little groups and there was no proper focus. I wanted to run away.

Peter obviously noticed the expression of alarm on my face.

'What's wrong, Marie?' he asked.

'The first thing I'm going to have to do is set down a routine here,' I explained.

'That's why I brought you here, Marie,' he said.

'There may be some problems with the parents, Peter,' I warned.

'Leave that to me,' he said firmly.

The first rule I introduced was to exclude parents from the class. When you have parents there, the dancers are distracted. Sometimes when you give an instruction, their eyes go to the parents. So the parents had to go, which didn't go down too well with them. The school was in Elizabeth city in New Jersey and it wasn't one of the best neighbourhoods. There were no coffee shops or facilities like that nearby where the parents could hang out, but I felt that wasn't my problem.

'I don't care where they go, but they're not staying here,' I insisted to Peter.

So when that was sorted, I called the class to order and told the young American kids that while we were working nobody was to wander around the hall, and there was to be no talking. I could be the strict schoolmistress when I needed to be.

I ran a tight ship, but then that's how I got results. And Peter Smith, his pupils and their parents saw the results over the next few years when they became the top school there.

Then I went on to Maureen Hall in Denver, Colorado. Maureen had been in the McTaggart school in Cork before she emigrated. We really hit it off at the workshops. And when the work was done, we'd go on shopping sprees together, as us ladies do. I also worked with the Julie Showalter School in Chicago.

I particularly enjoyed the social aspect to my time doing workshops in America. There were always lots of gatherings and sessions in different houses. Teacher and adjudicator Patsy McLoughlin's home in New Jersey was often the scene of some great music and craic. Patsy's husband Chris had a fabulous voice, so he would be singing all the great Irish songs of love and family and emigration, with the wines and beers flying to add to the merriment.

It was great fun.

My schools kept growing, with requests coming in from all over North America from teachers like Ann Richens, Mary McGing, Helen Gannon, Patricia Kennelly and the Trinity School, Chicago and the Healys.

Then Australia opened up to me. I had done workshops there for Cathie Cosgriff and Liz Finn Howe when I was in Inis Ealga, so that established the contacts. After hearing that I had my own school, Cathie asked me over to teach at her school in Melbourne, and I had similar requests from Liz, and from Jackie Miller in Adelaide.

I continued doing the workshops with Cathie in Melbourne, right up to the time I joined Michael Flatley when he started work on *Lord of the Dance*. Cathie would also regularly come to this side of the world and we developed a lifelong friendship. She even joined me when I celebrated my seventieth birthday with family and friends in December 2015, at Tylney Hall Hotel in Hampshire, England.

I enjoyed my regular visits to Melbourne and it was rewarding to see the Cosgriff school grow and grow into one of Australia's top schools, winning all the categories at the Australian championships in solos, céilí and figure choreography; and also seeing one of her dancers, Conor Hayes, starting out as a young lad and growing up to win the world's men's championship. Conor went on to become a lead dancer in *Riverdance*. What was so gratifying about doing continuous workshops was witnessing the development of the dancers and the school and making lifelong friends.

The Marie Duffy School had now gone international – much to the delight and pride of my mother.

ME AND MY MUM

Mother and I shared some very happy years together after we bought the bungalow in Kinsealy. We were great company for each other.

Although I'd leave her behind when I'd go off to America every summer to do my workshops, I always set aside a week for us to have a holiday together in some exotic location when I returned. We'd go to the south of Spain, and Greece was another of her favourite places in the sun. There were some wonderful holidays together in Ireland as well.

Mum was a big fan of Wicklow, or 'The Garden of Ireland' as that county is known because of its breathtaking beauty. She loved nothing more than a drive around the gorgeous Wicklow countryside in my little car, crawling up narrow, winding mountain roads and rolling slowly down into picturesque valleys, taking in the stunning vistas and booking into quaint hotels along the way.

It was a lovely time in our lives and I'd never seen Mum happier.

My school continued to flourish, and Mum took an active interest in it, getting to know all the pupils and following their progress in competitions. I kept the numbers small because I wanted to give each dancer equal attention and coaching to help them work to their strengths. I tailor-made dances to suit them. My aim, as always, was to produce quality dancers.

Of course, I knew that some children were never going to be great dancers. But I never turned away a child for that reason. I still took the child under my wing, and did as much as I could with them. That took time and patience. I had to be sensitive and diplomatic in those individual cases because it's so easy to damage a child's confidence. I gave them constructive criticism, always stressing the positive aspects of what they were doing, while letting them know gently that some steps just didn't suit them.

It was quite tricky dealing with parents as well because, naturally, they want the best for their child, and they want their children to get the breaks in life. I had to be diplomatic in the way I handled delicate situations with the parents as well as the children.

Sometimes you'd find dancers with great natural ability and see them squander their talent because they were lazy. My experience is that the dancers who had to work hard to achieve their potential were the ones who got the best results.

But I always encouraged children, irrespective of their ability, to enjoy their dancing. It had to be fun in order for them to love it and to have the passion for it. And I firmly believe that Irish dancing is a great experience for a child in terms of developing good life skills. They learn discipline, control, how to take direction, teamwork and how to cope with the ups and downs of life, the losing as well as the winning. The children learn to conquer their fears and it builds their confidence.

And, believe me, it takes a lot of confidence to step on to a stage in front of a hall full of people.

For some, Irish dancing would become their life's work as teachers, because they had found their vocation. Not all teachers were great champions in their own right, but champions don't always make good teachers. Some just don't have the patience for it. A lot of time and perseverance goes into teaching. My experience is that dancers who grew up loving it, even if they weren't exceptional winners, often went on to run some of the best schools around the world.

Mum travelled to all the feiseanna around the country after I started my own school, spending those weekends away from home with me. Each day she'd take her seat in the venue, and you could see the excitement on her face as my dancers were performing. She was a great woman for prayer, and she'd be praying that the dancers would do well. But mostly, I think, her prayers and her rosaries were for me to get a man. I know she would have been delighted to see me find somebody because I'm sure it was on her mind that, now that she was in her eighties, time was running out for her, and she wanted to see me married before that moment arrived.

At this stage, I was nicely settled in my lifestyle and it didn't bother me that there was no partner in my life. I had a nice group of close friends, both male and female; in fact, my best friend was a male, but it was a purely platonic relationship. So I was quite happy and had everything sorted, as I thought. And I loved the fact that my school was a great social outlet for my mother at that time, particularly as she was in the twilight years of her life.

* * *

My relationship with my mother hadn't always been so good. Although she had been unselfish, making so many personal sacrifices to give me a top-class education and to equip me with good social skills during my childhood and teenage years, Mum then became quite needy and demanding when I was in my twenties, thirties and even my forties. As her only daughter, I was the family member she clung to for attention.

There were times when it was very difficult for me to get away from her.

I got an anonymous phone call on one occasion during the early years of my adult life, and it was a female voice on the other end saying, 'I've found your mother on the street, she has collapsed.'

I recognised the disguised voice: it was Mum making the call. Her attention-seeking left me baffled.

Another time I had arranged to go with friends to the traditional horse racing festival at Leopardstown on St Stephen's Day. On the morning of the event, Mum suddenly took ill and asked me to call an ambulance. She was rushed to hospital and I feared the worst.

A nurse, noticing how distraught I was, took me aside in the hospital later that day and told me to go home.

'We have seen your mother get out of bed, carefully slide down the wall on to the floor and call for help. There is nothing wrong with her,' she said.

I was absolutely shocked. It was very difficult to reconcile this bizarre behaviour with the strong, independent woman who had reared me. Sometimes the pressure of dealing with her would be so bad that I'd have to call Seamas and get him to come and rescue me. Seamas would give her a good talking-to, and then I would get the silent treatment from her for days afterwards.

When old age set in, as so often happens in the circle of life, the parent eventually becomes the child, and the child is thrust into the position of the carer. And that's how it went with us. But she was much easier to deal with at this stage, probably because we were now living together and she had that security. And, to be fair, she was encouraging me to find myself a partner, even though I was quite happy on my own.

* * *

Coming up to her eightieth birthday, I planned a lovely family get-together to celebrate that milestone in Mum's life. The boys came home from England, but she took a sudden turn before the celebrations and was rushed to hospital. So that birthday party never happened. This time she was genuinely ill, and we were so relieved when she recovered and returned home following a few weeks of treatment.

Two years later, Mum was back in Beaumont Hospital after collapsing at home. She was unconscious by the time she arrived at the hospital, and the medical staff told me there was a possibility she would not come out of it. I immediately contacted the family in England, and they made arrangements to come home as quickly as possible. Meanwhile, I maintained a vigil at her bedside that first night.

When my brother Brian arrived the following afternoon he saw the exhausted condition I was in. In the evening, he urged me to go home and sleep, insisting that he would stay with Mum. There had been no change in her condition either way. Kinsealy was close by, and I was so shattered at this stage that I agreed to his suggestion.

Early the next morning I woke up to the sound of my doorbell ringing. When I opened it, Brian was standing on the step. My heart jumped with fright, thinking my mother had died in the night.

'You're not going to belive this,' Brian said, breaking into a smile.

'She's sitting up in bed having her breakfast!'

There were several serious incidents of this nature over a few years, where she would somehow bounce back from death's door. The sad thing is, while Mum's body was breaking down, her mind was as sharp as ever. We'd always watch the news programmes on TV together to keep ourselves up to speed on what was happening in the world. Mum was totally aware of everything that was going on in politics globally as well as at home, and she'd be giving me her own opinions on the current affairs.

If my mother was ill when any of the dancing competitions were taking place, as happened a couple of times, I would stay with her. There would be other championships, but my mother wasn't going to be around forever.

I never stayed to mind her out of a sense of obligation.

I wanted to be with her.

* * *

My mother was in Beaumont Hospital when the World Championships came around in Easter 1991. The city of Limerick was hosting the event that year. Mum was making a good recovery in hospital and I had no concerns about her. We discussed the World Championships, and she insisted that I should go. She had been due to leave hospital that weekend.

'I'll wait till you come back from Limerick,' she said.

So that was the plan. I told her I'd be back on the Sunday night.

'I'll come home on Monday or Tuesday,' Mum told me.

Although she wasn't seriously ill or incapacitated, I arranged for a carer to be with her at the house for the following week when I would go to work.

Mum was happy with that.

I stopped by to see her in the hospital on the Saturday morning before I set off on my journey down to Limerick. She was in great spirits and she named off all the children from my school who were competing in the World Championships and asked me to give them her best wishes.

She was in such good form that I felt very comfortable leaving her for the weekend.

That Saturday evening in Limerick I met up for dinner with one of my close friends, Brendan. On the Sunday morning we went to the venue and I prepped the kids for the competition that was about to start. Then I saw Terry Gillan walking down through the hall, flanked by two members of the Gardaí in uniform. I wonder what's wrong, I thought. Next I noticed Terry beckoning over my friend Brendan. I feared then that there had been some kind of a serious incident at the championships.

Seconds later Brendan came over to me looking very solemn.

'Marie, there's an urgent message to call your brother, Seamas; your mother has taken a turn,' he said.

I immediately rushed over to the hotel, but it didn't cross my mind that she had gone.

It was Seamas who broke the news to me. Mum had died an hour earlier. Staff at the hospital told my other brother, Brian, that her passing was very sudden.

She had just closed her eyes and slipped away.

It was a terrible shock to me because there had been no warning. She had been on top form when I left. Afterwards, when I had time to take it in, I came to the conclusion that Mum had somehow known her time was near, and she'd deliberately sent me away to make it easier on both of us.

* * *

As soon as the news filtered out in Limerick, I was surrounded by my second family, the people in Irish dancing who where there for the World Championships. The Irish dancing crowd are very competitive, but anytime anyone is in trouble and needs help they are the first to rally round and support each other. And that's the way it was with me. All the teachers who were there from around the world had been busy up to that moment preparing their dancers for the competitions, but they immediately dropped everything and came to see me.

One of my friends, Isabella, then stepped back from her adjudicating duties and took over the responsibility of looking after all the young people from my school, while Brendan drove me back to Dublin. My two friends from Chicago, Laverne and Patrick Showalter, whose daughter, Julie, I had taught on a one-to-one basis in America, also accompanied me on the sad journey back to Dublin.

I will never forget the kindness of everyone at that time.

In life, Mum had never been on a stage, but we gave her a send-off fit for a star. We organised a beautiful funeral Mass, and the church in Kinsealy was packed with family, neighbours and old friends from all over the globe.

Then we took Mother on her final journey through her beloved city of Dublin, crossing the River Liffey as the cortège made it's way to the south side, where we laid her to rest alongside my father in Mount Jerome Cemetery at Harold's Cross.

In the aftermath, when everyone had gone back to their own lives and I was left to grieve alone, it was hard to believe that she was gone.

However, I had the consolation of knowing that, despite our ups and downs, there were no regrets; nothing had been left unsaid.

Mum knew that I loved her.

And I do believe that Mum had a hand in what happened next …

THE MYSTERY MAN

Waiting at the check-in desk for a red-eye flight out of New-castle in the UK on a dark, chilly February morning in 1992, I noticed a distinguished-looking gent heading my way.

I remember thinking: 'Now, there's a very handsome man!'

It was just after 4.30 a.m. and I was the first and only person in the queue. There was nobody on duty at the check-in as it hadn't opened. The airport was almost deserted at that moment, apart from the two of us and a few people here and there.

The good-looking, smartly dressed stranger with a head of beautiful silver hair stopped at the desk where I was standing and then sidled up beside me.

'It's not open yet,' I said in a tone that staked my claim to pole position in the queue.

My opening salvo broke the ice. We introduced ourselves to each other and got chatting.

'Ian Messenger is my name,' the stranger said.

We made some chit-chat and then, as the conversation developed, Ian told me that he was going through a bereavement. His wife, Iris, had died suddenly a month earlier while waiting for a lung transplant.

I could see that Ian was absolutely heartbroken; the tears were welling up as he spoke. Although our circumstances were different, I could also empathise with the pain he was going through, having lost my mother the previous year.

I would later learn that Ian and Iris had enjoyed a blissfully happy marriage, and had reared a son and daughter, Barry and Lynda. Then their world came apart when Iris was diagnosed with a lung disease some years earlier. Ian had remained totally devoted to Iris as they battled through this horrible period in their lives.

On the morning I met him, Ian had taken time off from his job to mend his shattered life, and was heading abroad to spend some time with his friends, Paul and Ruth Meyn, in Kansas, USA. The early part of Ian's working life had been spent in the British army. When he retired from the army, Ian then found employment with the Newcastle regional government where he was then working in the housing department as chief procurement officer.

Something else had happened to Ian that broke him completely in the immediate aftermath of Iris' passing. They had a lovely poodle called Lady that they both adored. Lady was like another human being in their family, as people who own dogs or other pets will understand. Ian lived in a place called Prudhoe outside Newcastle, and a week earlier, while they were out walking, Lady ran on to a road and was struck by a passing car. The little dog died in Ian's arms at the side of the ditch.

Losing his pet, and this very tangible connection with Iris, was just too much to bear. Ian decided to take off. That morning he was flying to Manchester to catch a connecting flight to Kansas.

As we finally checked in and waited to board our flight on that wintry morning, Ian asked if I would be returning to Newcastle at any point in the future.

I had told Ian about my work as an Irish dancing teacher, explaining that I had been over to do a workshop.

'Actually, I think I'm coming back in a couple of months,' I said in reply to his question.

'Maybe I could take you out for a pizza then,' Ian suggested.

'Yes, that would be lovely,' I told him.

I had only known him for an hour, but already I felt very comfortable in Ian's company.

Then we exchanged our home phone numbers before going our separate ways.

* * *

The strange aspect to meeting Ian is that I shouldn't have been in the airport that morning.

One of my longtime friends Mary Lyndsay McMaster, an Irish dancing teacher and adjudicator from Newcastle, had asked me if I would be interested in doing a workshop there for a local dancing school run by a lady called Barbara Slator. It's an easy journey from Dublin to Newcastle, so I took up the offer.

On my first weekend trip over in November of that year, 1991, I brought along one of my dancers, Derval O'Brien, to demonstrate the steps.

Barbara Slator's class turned out to be a very talented group of dancers, and many of them would later end up in *Lord of the Dance*. Barbara asked me back the following February, and this time I was on my own.

As I was going to be in Newcastle for only a couple of days, I decided to travel light with a carry-on bag. I went over on the Friday, and my return journey was Sunday evening on an Aer Lingus flight. We did classes until the afternoon on the Sunday, and then I went for a bite to eat and a good chat with Barbara in one of the airport hotels before the flight.

I was in a very relaxed mood because Newcastle is a very small airport and I knew that I didn't have to check in until an hour beforehand, especially as I had a carry-on bag. Eventually I said goodbye to Barbara and went off to get my flight home after a very fruitful weekend with the young dancers.

I was on top form as I approached the Aer Lingus desk. I gave the person on duty my ticket, and produced my passport.

The young ground stewardess checked my details, and I could see her smiley face change to a look of concern.

'I'm sorry,' she said after a long pause. 'I'm afraid you don't have a seat.'

'What do you mean?' I asked, confident that she was making a mistake.

'I'm afraid your seat has been allocated to another passenger,' she informed me.

At this point I could feel anger welling up inside me.

'How could that happen?' I blurted out, incredulously.

'We thought you weren't coming, so we gave it away,' she explained, shuffling in her seat.

I tapped my ticket on the counter, insisting, 'I have a ticket that's bought and paid for; how could you give my seat to somebody else? I was here in plenty of time, I'm totally within the rules, and I have carry-on luggage.'

Clockwise from top left: My grandmother Duffy; my father, Joe Duffy (standing at the back), pictured as best man at his friend's wedding; my eldest brother, Owen; my mother, Mary.

Above: Here I am, second from left, at an All-Ireland Championship.

Below: I'm standing on the left beside the Inis Ealga Senior World Figure Dance Champions.

Right: My student Emma Jane Lavin winning one of her many World Championships. The sponsor handing over the plaque is my good friend Laverne Showalter.

Below: Ian and me on our wedding day, 18 August 1991. We got married in Kansas, and Julie Showalter, daughter of Laverne (above) was my bridesmaid.

Above: Backstage at the opening night of *Lord of the Dance* in the Point in the summer of 1996.

Below: With Michael in his dressing room at the 1997 Oscars, and with Ian on the red carpet outside.

Above: The original cast of *Lord of the Dance*, pictured during our record-breaking run at Wembley Arena in 1997. At the back, behind Ronan and Michael, are promoter Harvey Goldsmith and Derek MacKillop from Michael's management company at the time (John Reid Enterprises). In the front row, with the blonde hair, is violinist Máiréad Nesbitt, and front right is 'Erin the Goddess' Anne Buckley.

Here I am with Damien O'Kane and Bernadette Flynn, the two leads from *Lord of the Dance* who would go on to get married and set up a dancing school together.

Left and below: During rehearsals for *Feet of Flames* in 1998, with 'Little Spirit' Helen Egan and 'Erin the Goddess' Anne Buckley.

Below: Michael and me with the second *Lord of the Dance* troupe, rehearsing for the American tour.

Then I began to panic.

'When is the next flight?' I asked.

'I'm afraid this is the last one out of Newcastle tonight,' she told me in an apologetic tone.

Now I really felt a sense of panic.

'I have to get to Dublin tonight. I have a very important job at nine in the morning,' I insisted, telling a little white lie.

I usually kept Monday mornings free, but I didn't want all the hassle of staying in Newcastle that night, and having to get up in the middle of the night for an early morning flight the following day.

'I'm afraid our first flight doesn't leave until nine tomorrow morning,' the stewardess then informed me.

Now that I had worked myself up to a state of indignation, I insisted that I had to be in Dublin for my meeting at nine in the morning and I refused to budge until I got a satisfactory solution from the airline.

After some further checking and conferring with a colleague, the stewardess then gave me the option of staying in a nearby hotel overnight at the airline's expense, then taking a flight to Manchester at six in the morning to catch a connecting flight to Dublin, where I would be in lots of time for my 9 a.m. meeting.

'Okay, that's fine,' I said.

As I walked out of the airport to the hotel, the thought suddenly struck me.

'What have I done! I don't need to be in Dublin at nine. Now I have to get up in the middle of the night to get the first of two flights.'

Be careful what you argue for!

And that's how I ended up being the first in line the following morning for my flight to Manchester ... when Ian Messenger walked into my life.

Strange coincidences happen, but later Ian and I would say that perhaps

Iris and my mother had a hand in my being bumped off the flight the previous night.

* * *

In the immediate aftermath of my mother's death, I finally decided that the time was right for a move to America. It had been Mum's wish for me in my early adult life, but I didn't have the courage or the conviction at that time to take the leap out of my life in Ireland. I had never given up on the idea, so now the time felt right for me to start afresh in the States.

I had lots of connections there, of course, from doing Chicago workshops with the Showalters, and with Trinity, a big school run by Mark Howard. I had also worked with Maureen Hall in California, Peter Smith in New Jersey, Mary McGing in Cincinnati, Ann Richens in Daton, Ohio and at Helen Gannon's school in St Louis. Helen was born and raised in Limerick city where she grew up learning Irish dancing with a lady called Mrs LeGeer. When Helen got married, she emigrated to St Louis in 1967 with her physician husband, P.J., and went on to become the first commissioned Irish dance instructor in the state of Missouri, and a huge figure in Comhaltas over there.

It was Helen who said to me that if I was interested in applying for a visa to America she would help me through the cultural sources there. As I was financially independent and well able to support myself in a career in the world of Irish dancing, Helen didn't foresee any obstacle to me being granted a visa. So I went through the whole process, doing the red tape, filling in all the forms from the American Embassy, getting my medical examination, and everything else that goes with it. I was then expecting to get my final clearance in April of that year, 1992.

* * *

A few weeks later I came home from an evening dance class in Dublin, and there was a message on my phone. It was a voicemail from Ian, which began by reminding me that we had met in the airport.

'I'm just wondering if you are coming back to Newcastle, or maybe I'll take a weekend trip to Dublin as I've never been,' he said.

I wouldn't say my heart skipped a beat, though I was quite excited to hear his voice. But to be honest, I hadn't given my encounter with Ian at Newcastle Airport much thought when I returned home as I was so caught up in my work, and my mind was also in a whirl about starting a new life in America.

When I returned Ian's phone call, the conversation flowed easily, like we were old friends. At the end of it, we had arranged to meet up in Dublin. I suggested the nearest hotels to where I was living in the city.

This was my way of setting the ground rules, keeping it formal because, really, Ian was a stranger to me. He booked the Skylon Hotel, which is not very far from Dublin Airport, and came over the following weekend.

The time just flew in Dublin that weekend with Ian. He was a great conversationalist, interesting, attentive, entertaining and with a great sense of humour. Ian was also a very good listener.

I really enjoyed his company over those couple of days, and the feeling was mutual. I know this, because the next time I got a phone call after he returned home, Ian asked me to marry him!

I didn't see the proposal coming and I was speechless on the other end of the line. 'Hello, hello …' Ian said.

'Yes, I'm still here,' I told him, not knowing what else to say.

Eventually I spluttered, 'We don't know each other very long.'

Ian was confident. 'I've always made up my mind very quickly on things that I know are right,' he explained.

He told me that it had been the same with Iris. Ian knew very quickly that they had been right for each other. Now he felt the same about me.

I didn't say yes straight away, but neither did I turn him down. There was something about this man that intrigued me. I believe I have good instincts, and my impression of Ian, in the short period of getting to know him, was all good. He was a lovely, kind, gentle man. And, of course, very easy on the eye.

I went over to Newcastle and spent some time with Ian. He introduced me to his friends and work colleagues, all of whom were decent, friendly, welcoming people. I could see that they were all so fond of Ian, which was no surprise considering his lovely nature. And very quickly I formed the same opinion as Ian: that the relationship felt so right.

After waiting a lifetime, I felt I had nothing to lose.

'Okay, let's go for it,' I finally told Ian in reply to his proposal.

This was coming up to the World Championships, so it was within a year of my mother passing away.

I truly believe that she did her little job.

* * *

In the meantime, I was notified that my American visa had been approved. I just had to do the final trip out to the States to sign off on it. Even though events were now moving very fast in my personal life, I decided to keep my options open. So I headed off across the Atlantic in March and got my visa to work in America.

When I returned to Ireland, I was immediately caught up in all the demands of the World Championships, which were being held in Limerick again that year.

At this stage, I still hadn't confided in any of my close circle of friends about Ian because there had been so much going on at the speed of a Grand Prix race.

Down at the World Championships in Limerick, I received a call from Ian to say that he was travelling over to Dublin to see me. I arranged with my brother Seamas to go and pick him up at the airport and take care of him until I got back a day later. It was during this visit that Ian suggested we should explore the city's jewellery shops for an engagement ring, an expedition that concluded with the purchase of my sparkler.

Now that I had made an official commitment to Ian, it was time to tell my family and all my friends in the world of dance near and far.

You can imagine the shock waves among my friends at home and abroad. They had waited for decades to hear that I had found someone to share my life with. Then they had assumed, as I did, that I'd missed the boat to find a husband. Now here I was, in my middle age, announcing out of the blue that I was getting married to a man nobody had ever met, or even heard about!

I'm sure that some people harboured concerns for a time about the turn my life was taking, but that would have been out of love for me. Once people met Ian and the word spread about the lovely man in my life, any worries people had about the 'mystery man' instantly went away.

Once I had accepted Ian's proposal and the ring had been purchased, we both agreed to marry at the earliest opportunity. I joked to friends that I was now forty-seven years old, so time wasn't on my side. I also said I wanted to make sure this fella didn't get away. It was a very exciting time and I had a lot of fun with it.

I never thought for one moment that organising a church wedding would then spoil my party.

WEDDING BLUES

AND RIVERDANCE

My mother's prayers had been answered the day Ian asked me to marry him; I know she was smiling down on me at that moment.

In life, Mum was religious and, as I mentioned earlier, she believed in the power of prayer. Both of us had been regular churchgoers in Kinsealy during the period that we lived there together. And we were known to the local priests, as they visited my mother when she was ill.

Ian and myself decided that we would get married there in August, which would be six months after our first encounter in Newcastle Airport. As I was living in Kinsealy, my dream was to have my wedding ceremony in the lovely local church.

Ian wasn't a member of the Catholic faith, but he had expressed his wish to convert. He had never been baptised. As the youngest of a very large family, Ian's parents had given him the option of choosing his religion when he was old enough to make that decision.

I went up to the priests' house in Kinsealy to book in a date and make arrangements for our wedding.

The priest, a man in his forties, looked concerned when I told him that I wanted to get married as soon as possible. This priest had been to my home numerous times visiting my mother when she was sick and of course he would have noticed that there wasn't a man around the place that I was likely to wed. But I remember laughing to myself: 'Surely to God he doesn't think I'm pregnant and this is a shotgun wedding at my age!'

The priest strutted around the room and he got more agitated as every second passed.

'This is all very sudden – who is this man you are going to marry?' he eventually asked.

I filled him in on Ian's background, explaining that he was a widower who had lost his wife in recent times.

'Well,' he said, 'before we progress with this, I'd like to meet him.'

At this stage I accepted that the church had its own rules and regulations and that, perhaps, the priest was looking after my best interests.

So, after that conversation, I informed Ian that the priest would like to meet with him, and he said he was happy to do that on his next visit.

That encounter between the priest and Ian did not go well.

The priest, it transpired, was totally opposed to the marriage. Two of the reasons he put forward were: we barely knew each other, and it was too soon after Ian's bereavement.

'Why should Ian have to go through it alone?' I argued.

I was very upset and I implored the priest to allow us to marry in the church.

'There is no impediment: the man is a widower, I'm a single woman, and he is willing to convert to Catholicism,' I insisted.

'He doesn't have to convert, I just don't think it's right,' the priest responded.

I thought, well, who are you to be making that decision for me!

This was also a red rag to a bull for Ian, who then had a heated argument with the priest, with both losing their temper.

'I wouldn't take you into our church,' the priest said at one point.

'Well, I wouldn't want to be in there now,' Ian shot back.

I took Ian by the arm and we both marched out.

I was left shaken by the experience and the priest's attitude, which had taken me completely by surprise.

My brother Brian was working in a priory in the Dublin suburb of Templeogue at the time. I went to see Brian and told him what had happened.

'I have every right to be married in my own church, don't I Brian?' I added, still quite emotional.

Brian agreed with me. He said he would discuss it with the hierarchy in the priory.

Sure enough, Brian came back to me with the news that they could find no reason why the marriage should not be allowed in the church.

I was very disillusioned with the Church, or rather the individual priest who was blocking my wedding. Luckily, I was about to go to America to do one of my workshops, so I knew that getting out of Ireland for a short time would be good for my head.

I was due to travel to the States on my own, but then Ian offered to go with me, saying we could get married in a ceremony while we were over there. As we talked it over, Ian suggested that we should go on to Kansas, where his friends, Paul and Ruth Meyn, would help us make all the arrangements.

I thought that was an absolutely wonderful idea.

And the cloud lifted.

Paul and Ruth welcomed me into their home in Bonner Springs, a sleepy city in Kansas, and I fell in love with the couple straight away. Even though I was a newcomer to Ian's life, particularly so soon after the passing of Iris, they embraced me and treated me like an old friend.

They introduced us to a local church. It wasn't a Catholic religion, but what was important to us was the fact that we were going to have a ceremony where our marriage would be blessed in front of people we both loved and respected, those who could make the trip down for this special moment in our lives.

The fact that the wedding was in America meant that lots of my friends from the Irish dancing world in the US were in a position to travel to Kansas. Peter Smith, my dear, dear friend who has since passed away, flew in from New Jersey to give me away. When I asked him weeks beforehand to do me that honour he leapt with joy as he instantly accepted. On the day of my wedding the smile on Peter's face was like the cat who got the cream.

Laverne Showalter came in from Chicago with her husband Patrick and their daughter Julie, who was my bridesmaid.

Other American friends who joined us included Patsy McLoughlin and Fidelma Davis from New Jersey; Mary McGing; Ann Richens; and Helen Gannon, who runs Comhaltas in St Louis, was there with her husband P.J.

There were also lots of American friends from Ian's life, people he had grown close to during his visits to Paul and Ruth.

The ceremony on the day was a very simple, gorgeous affair, with little children playing the harp. My friend Orfhlaith Ní Bhriain was over on tour in America and she sang at the ceremony, which was just magical because Orfhlaith sings like an angel.

As I stood facing Ian, looking into his eyes while he asked me to be his wife, I had never been more certain about any decision I had made in my life.

I knew that I wanted to spend the rest of my days with this man.

Afterwards, we had a very traditional Irish party. There was singing and dancing as the beer and wine flowed, with lots of laughter and great banter filling the air. It would have been lovely to have had my family there to complete the otherwise perfect day, but I knew that we would celebrate with them when we returned to Dublin.

While I was out of the country marrying my Prince Charming, my brother Brian had been pursuing my case through the fathers in the priory where he worked. They wrote to the Archbishop of Dublin asking for an explanation as to why I had been refused my wedding in the Kinsealy parish. The response that came back was positive. The Archbishop confirmed that there was no reason to prevent me from proceeding with my wedding in the Catholic Church.

Even though the moment had been spoiled by the row with my local priest over the matter, I was thrilled when we eventually had our Catholic wedding ceremony in a Dublin church with all my family around me, and lots more friends. Ian and I took our vows again, this time in a little church at Dublin Airport. Neither of us had wanted to return to Kinsealy, the scene of all the unnecessary fuss and, indeed, heartache.

Having waited until I was a middle-aged woman before the right man came along and swept me off my feet, I then married Ian for the second time.

To be sure, to be sure, you could say.

* * *

Marriage may have come late in my life, but my goodness it was worth the wait. Ian was the most wonderful man. Caring, considerate, selfless and strong, he was totally devoted to me from the moment we began our life together.

I was still teaching Irish dancing in Dublin schools, as well as running my own dance school, when we got married.

Ian, who was fifteen years older than me, decided to take early retirement and he encouraged me to continue with my Irish dancing work. We spent our time flitting between my home in Kinsealy and his house in the lovely olde worlde English village of Prudhoe, Northumberland, about six miles outside Newcastle.

Even though he was English with no knowledge of the Irish dancing scene up to that point, Ian embraced it straight away. He was a very intelligent, open-minded man and eagerly soaked up the culture.

And, my God, he had the patience of a saint!

There was one particular day when I was judging competitions from early morning until late at night. Ian sat through it all, occasionally supplying me with cups of tea. It didn't bother him how long he had to sit there on one of the most uncomfortable chairs in the world. There wasn't a single word of complaint from Ian. He was just totally devoted.

Ian came to all the big events with me, and he'd always say to me, 'If I can be of any help in any way I'm happy to do it.'

On one such occasion, Ian did get a job doing a long shift on the door, taking care of the administration, sending people in the right direction, and answering a million questions from the dance groups that came through. When I took over, Ian then sat with me. He was a perfect gentleman and made me so happy.

However, my joy turned to devastation when the then treasurer of the Irish dancing Coimisiún called me aside late into the event and said that another member had complained about Ian being there and wanted him removed.

'Why does he have a problem with Ian being here?' I asked, suddenly feeling queasy and shaky with shock.

'It's because he was a soldier in the British army,' came the reply.

For a second I could barely catch my breath as the words sunk in and cut me to the bone. Never for a moment had I thought that Ian's early career in the army would have been an issue in any part of my life, but particularly Irish dancing. The person who made the complaint was from the North of Ireland. But Ian had never served there. He'd been in Malta and in army bases around England and Germany. And anyway, he wasn't at all political.

Ian absolutely loved Ireland, the people, the culture and now he was even as passionate about Irish dancing as I was myself. I was so hurt and disgusted to hear that someone on the Coimisiún didn't want Ian to be involved with us. This was in the early nineties and I couldn't believe that such a bias still existed.

'Okay, I don't want Ian to know anything about this because he would be so hurt,' I said after eventually composing myself.

Instead, I removed myself from my duties at the event and we left. My only consolation is that Ian was none the wiser as to why I finished earlier than expected.

Thankfully, it never happened again.

* * *

As sugary as it sounds, we were both blissfully happy in our marriage. Ian enjoyed living with me in Kinsealy, and I loved the regular visits to his cosy house in Prudhoe. However, after the initial novelty of going back and forth between Ireland and England, we both agreed that it was unnecessary hassle running two homes. I then decided that it was time for me to move on and finally make a complete break with Dublin. We put the Kinsealy house on the market and it sold within a short period.

When I was clearing out my home in Kinsealy, two friends, Terry and Philip, offered their services with the packing and removal of furniture and other belongings that I planned to take with me to England.

While sifting through all the bits and pieces, Philip came across the old bridal doll that I had been given as a present by my sister-in-law Lena in England when I was a child. It was the doll that had belonged to my niece Joan, and it had been my pride and joy for years and years. By this stage it was black with dirt, so I said to Philip without a second thought: 'Throw it in the skip.'

Six months later, Philip came to visit me with a big smile on his face. Then he produced the doll from a bag, and I couldn't believe what I was seeing. Philip had taken her to the dolls' hospital in Dublin, and had her restored to her full glory. What a lovely thing to do! I was absolutely thrilled and, for the life of me, I couldn't believe the decision I had taken that day in Dublin to discard such a childhood treasure.

I'll put it down to the stress of moving.

After making my decision to move to the UK, I closed down The Marie Duffy School. Six months later several of my dancers from the school, as well as many I had worked with in Inis Ealga, were chosen by Michael Flatley at an open audition for the *Riverdance* spectacular in the 1994 Eurovision Song Contest.

* * *

The American country-rock band The Eagles have a song called 'Hotel California', which contains the line: 'You can check out any time you like, but you can never leave.' Irish dancing was a bit like that for me.

When I moved over to England I didn't have any ambition or plan to continue doing Irish dancing classes. But I had done workshops there with The Barbara Slator School in the past, and shortly after I arrived Barbara got in contact and invited me to work with her in the classes. I liked Barbara and we had become friends, so I took her up on the offer. The partnership worked out very well, as two years later Barbara's dancers got their highest world placings in céilí and figure choreography.

Then one morning I woke up and decided that Irish dancing was taking up a lot of my time again. I had moved over to be with Ian, so I decided to leave Barbara's school and retire from the scene. But, as before, you can never hang up your shoes in Irish dancing.

Danny Doherty, another good friend who runs a very successful school in the English midlands, then contacted me.

'Will you come down to the midlands and give me a bit of a hand?' Danny asked.

'Oh Danny, I'm seriously giving up,' I told him.

'Well, have a think about it, no pressure,' he said.

I talked it over with Ian, who, as ever, said he was happy to go along with whatever suited me. The classes weren't going to be a full week, so I agreed to give it a trial.

You can check out any time you like, but you can never leave!

The classes started on a Thursday evening, then into Friday and Saturday, and I would return home on the Sunday.

Ian and I travelled to Coventry by car every week and stayed over at Danny's house. Ian was a fantastic driver, but we had some hairy moments on those journeys. Thanks to his skill behind the wheel, Ian saved us both from being killed on one occasion when we met a lorry on our side of the road and almost ended up in a head-on crash. Ian avoided the collision and certain death by swerving on to the other side. Fortunately, there was nothing coming from that direction at the time. We were both left shaken by the experience, but thanked our lucky stars that it obviously wasn't our time.

* * *

Shortly after the stunning success of the seven-minute *Riverdance* interval act in the 1994 Eurovision Song Contest, producer Moya Doherty decided to weave it out into a major stage show, with Michael Flatley creating and choreographing the dances for the storyline.

Riverdance, the show, opened at The Point in Dublin on 5 February 1995, and ran for five weeks before moving on to The Apollo in Hammersmith, London, in May of that year.

Some of my dancers who were involved in the Eurovision performance that night had been telling me all about the show. It was very exciting stuff, and I suggested to Ian that we should book tickets for The Apollo.

'I really have to go see this,' I said.

Ian was just as enthusiastic.

We had Kelly Breen, an Irish dancer from Melbourne, Australia, staying with us at the time. So I booked for the three of us to go and see a pre-view show, and we took the train down from Newcastle. When we arrived, I decided to get a few cards to wish the dancers I'd worked with good luck on their big night. They included Frieda Gray, a gorgeous girl from Ballymun in Dublin who was one of my early world champions, as were her two sisters, Muiread and Maria. It was unusual to have three members of the same family winning many World Championships. The Conlon family from Clontarf in Dublin also achieved this feat and four of them were All-Ireland champions.

My dancers in the show also included Tracey Taaffe, sisters Niamh and Aoibheann O'Brien, and Niamh and Sinead O'Connor.

And, of course, I knew all of the dancers on the famous *Riverdance* line from the Eurovision.

I got my cards and headed off down to The Apollo to drop them off at the stage door. I didn't want to go in and meet the dancers in person because I knew it was a busy time for them.

As I strolled down a lane at the side of The Apollo, I spotted a man and a woman in the distance. I wasn't taking much notice of them as they drew nearer. But as they stepped smartly past me, I realised that the male was Michael Flatley.

I turned around and Michael was swivelling at the same time.

'Marie Duffy!' he declared.

'How are you Michael!' I said, as he wrapped me in his arms and gave me a big hug.

I'll never forget his words as he then introduced me to Moya Doherty.

'This is Marie Duffy, the best dance teacher in the world, and the best dancers we have in there on the line are hers.'

As we talked, I explained to Michael that I was just dropping in some good luck cards to my dancers. Michael insisted on sending for dance captain Frieda Gray, who arrived out full of joy and excitement, and accompanied by several other dancers known to me.

They were jumping up and down with glee and asking if I was going to the show that evening.

'Yes, yes, of course I'm going to be there to watch you,' I smiled.

Then, before I left, Michael said: 'Now, be sure and come back afterwards and have a glass of wine with us.'

'Yes, of course I will,' I said, although my intention was to slip away with Ian and Kelly after the performance.

As we were leaving the theatre in high spirits after the fabulous show that night, Frieda nabbed me. She had come out straight away to get me.

'You've got to come and have a glass of wine with us, Michael insists,' she said.

Well, there was no escape then, so we went in and mingled with everyone.

Frieda was the dance captain, and she took me aside and asked: 'How was it Marie? Can you give me a few tips?'

'I didn't come here to criticise, I came here to enjoy the show, and you were all fantastic,' I replied.

Frieda wasn't giving up. 'Marie, come on, you could be helping me with some ideas,' she insisted.

'Frieda, I don't need to, everything is fabulous.'

I wasn't telling a lie. The show was really impressive.

Frieda, however, continued to press me for a detailed critique. And eventually I relented. I talked through the performance in general with no big criticisms, but I did make some suggestions about where it could be tweaked here and there. So Frieda seemed quite happy with that.

Next, I saw Michael Flatley coming my way with a huge smile on his face.

'Well, Marie, what did you think?' he asked.

'It was fabulous, Michael,' I told him.

We clinked our wine glasses, chatted for a short time, and then he went off to mingle.

Michael was on top of the world that night.

But just a short time later that world would come tumbling down.

THE KID FROM CHICAGO

I had heard about Michael Flatley long before I ever set eyes on him. Even as a youngster, he was causing a stir, creating a legendary status.

'Oh, have you seen the kid from Chicago?'

That was the buzz going around the competitions across America about this local 'wonder kid' of Irish dancing.

When I was doing the workshops in America there would be a feis in places like Cleveland one weekend, and Buffalo the next. We'd all travel and gather at those feiseanna, and I began to hear the name Michael Flatley cropping up quite a lot.

He had created huge excitement among people who'd seen him dance.

I was intrigued by this young guy's reputation and was looking forward to the day I would see him dance.

* * *

It was his smiley face that first caught my attention when Michael was pointed out to me at a competition, as I finally got to watch him in action when he was about fourteen years old. He had gorgeous hair, laughing eyes and buckets of charm. Even before he took a step, I could see that this little guy had something special about him. In show business today, they call it the X factor. Whatever that is, it's a magic ingredient.

When Michael got up on stage that day, he charmed the judges. But he didn't have to use his words, because his feet did the talking.

I was just mesmerised watching him dance. He was way ahead of his time. Where everybody else was doing the solid rhythm and beat, Michael was performing syncopated stuff that had everybody asking, 'Where are those sounds coming from?' He only has one pair of feet, but it sounded like there were dozens of pairs hitting the floor. The sounds were coming from his toes, his heels, the middle of his shoes … all at the same time. He was amazing. I had never seen the like of it.

I remember meeting Michael later when I was over at another feis in America. Matt Meleady was with me, and as we were walking around the venue we bumped into Michael and his younger brother, Pat. They were two lovely, mannerly young guys.

'Hello, Mr Meleady,' Michael said.

Matt then introduced me to the two little lads, who seemed quite shy at the time, as young teens usually are.

They were both familiar with Inis Ealga because by then our school was a huge name in the competitive world of Irish dancing, as we had won every title going in every age group.

Our success would not have escaped Michael's attention. He would have seen the performances of our solo dancers and the huge number of titles that they won. He would also have seen our choreography and figure dancing, so I guess that's where Michael first noticed my work.

Later, he had many of my dancers in his first lineup with *Riverdance* at the Eurovision, and I know that he appreciated their training and he knew that I was the teacher who had trained them.

As a competitive dancer, Michael won numerous competitions in North America and Ireland, but it wasn't until 1975 that 'the kid from Chicago' finally became a world champion when he competed at the Mansion House in Dublin.

A frisson of excitement swept through the hall at the World Championships that year as word spread that 'the kid from Chicago' was competing for a top honour. The interest in young Michael Flatley was phenomenal.

You could hear people in corners and corridors asking: 'What time is this kid from Chicago on? What age group is he in?' and so on.

He was a superstar before he even appeared on stage that day.

Of course, Michael was going to be restricted in what he could do as a competitive dancer, having to dance to strict rhythm and time. There was a particular speed he had to adhere to. It was only in the set dance that he could do freestyle, but even then he had to keep his arms down by his side, which he obviously found really frustrating.

When Michael's dance came around, he was like a magnet drawing people from every nook and cranny in the building. Everybody piled into the hall to see this amazing kid that they'd either heard about or had seen at other competitions. It's not an exaggeration to say that he created electricity in the room.

And then a silence fell over the hall when he stepped up.

Michael's first dance was the light round, followed by a heavy dance, either a jig or a hornpipe. Then came the pièce de résistance, the freestyle set dance that he had choreographed himself. Jaws dropped as he took off like a rocket with his hands down by his sides. Rhythm-wise, whatever you could fit to the music was up to you. Well, what he did to the music nobody had ever seen before. He was so thrilling and mesmerising to watch. He made the straight arms, straight-looking dancing, look sexy. His feet were going at a hundred miles an hour. He was even doing moon walks. And when he finished it was probably one of the first times that somebody in competition got a standing ovation.

Even on that day, the teenage Michael Flatley was iconic.

Needless to say, the seven judges were equally blown away by Michael's performance, and Irish dancing had a new world champion.

Michael Flatley never danced in competition again to my knowledge. Once he had achieved his ultimate goal, the world champ moved on.

I heard some time later that he was running his own dance school in the Midwest of America.

The next time I met him, Michael was dancing with Irish traditional music superstars The Chieftains at the 1984 Special Olympics in Dublin. I was still with Inis Ealga and we'd been asked to put on an Irish dancing display at the event. This was a huge undertaking for us as we brought in all the other schools around Leinster, and we had about 200 dancers performing in different formations that day. We rehearsed the troupe a couple of times a week in the build up to the big event, and then we spent the day of the opening ceremony putting them through their paces at the venue for our massive exhibition of dancing.

Someone said to me on the day: 'The Chieftains are over on another stage and I hear that Michael Flatley is dancing with them.'

I decided to go looking for Michael, just to say hello.

It was springtime and the weather was very cold and wet as I made my way across to the stage where The Chieftains would be performing later. As luck would have it, Michael was there at that moment. He had matured in looks since I'd last seen him, but he still had the lovely hair and big, warm welcoming smile that I remembered.

Michael knew me straight off, and he gave me a big hug. As we were chatting I was shivering because I was underdressed for the biting cold of the day. Michael spotted my discomfort, and then the well-reared young gentleman took off a black leather jacket he was wearing and insisted that I put it on to warm up.

Later, I went over to see him dance with The Chieftains, and then he came over to watch our big display. We chatted some more afterwards, and I returned his leather jacket to him. And then we parted company with another big hug.

Michael always made you feel good when you were around him.

It was a decade later when I saw Michael again – this time he was on television, dancing at the interval of the 1994 Eurovision Song Contest in *Riverdance*. I was at home that night with Ian in our house on Western Avenue, Prudhoe. Although there had been a veil of secrecy around the *Riverdance* number at Eurovision, I knew there was a big performance coming up with some of the girls that I'd trained. Some of them told me, even though they weren't supposed to let out a whisper.

But I still wasn't prepared for what I saw.

As I sat and watched, I was filled with joy, but I also became a bit tearful because it had been only six months since I'd left some of those girls. They were my girls, and I was so proud of them as I snuggled up to Ian on our couch and watched the performance unfold on television.

Then Michael Flatley and Jean Butler exploded on to the stage in front of them and I got a jolt. I had never seen anything like that before in my life. It was sensational: a moment of magic that lit a fire and spread a love of Irish dancing around the globe. And it's still blazing to this day.

Michael put Irish dancing on the map worldwide that night, and even in Ireland itself.

There's now a feis in nearly every European country every weekend. Last year I was judging them myself in cities like Milan and Moscow.

And that's all down to the night Michael Flatley exploded on to the stage and became an overnight superstar at the 1994 Eurovision Song Contest.

* * *

What Michael and Jean did was completely new to me that night, but I was familiar with 'the line' because whenever Inis Ealga did big festivals around Europe we always performed a big line dance similar to *Riverdance*, except we did it to a hornpipe. Lily Comerford, who was a famous name in Dublin for Irish dancing going back to when I was a kid, always did a line too to end a big dance number, so that feature went back a long way. Lily, incidentally, was also famous for her black jackets and tan skirts.

I remember 'the line' serving us well when I was a young dance teacher with Inis Ealga and we were invited to represent Ireland at the Dijon Festival in France. The offer came from one of the Irish government departments, but we didn't realise how prestigious it was when we set off with our gang of about twenty young dancers.

Later we would discover that it was like the Olympics of folk dancing. In typical Irish fashion, we had to make our own way there, setting off with our suitcases in hand, carrying our gear and travelling by hackney cabs, train and boat. We eventually got there to find groups from every continent represented; they all had the ministers from their governments with them, and they were chauffeured around in big buses.

We didn't realise going out that it was a competition and that we were judged from the moment we arrived on several aspects, including our appearance, behaviour and performance.

I remember one very formal lunch attended by dignitaries where our group was completely baffled by the array of cutlery in front of us. We didn't know where to start or finish with them. As far as I can recall we were being judged on our knowledge of etiquette that day. I think we acquitted ourselves well enough, and the friendliness and good manners of the little Irish group seemed to go down very well.

Of course, we also had our secret 'weapon' with us: a tiny ten-year-old boy called Donal Conlon.

Little Donal was cute with lots of talent as a dancer. He caught the eye of every delegation from the get-go. In every venue we'd go to, the crowds starting chanting, 'Donal! Donal! Donal!' Donal had become famous very quickly for his 'clacks', as the locals called it. He was able to click his heels high up in the air. It was visually exciting to watch, so Donal instantly grew a fan club.

As the days went on, we realised from the headlines in the local newspapers that Ireland was getting great praise, with Donal's 'clacks' being singled out for mention. Whenever he would clack way above his head the crowd would go wild.

On the Sunday night, the final night of the festival, we were among the countries chosen to dance in the mega-concert. By now, we realised we were in a competition and it was serious business. This was both nerve-racking and exciting.

Every delegation had a guide, and our guy was so proud that his group had been doing so well up to then. That afternoon when we were given the order of our appearance on stage to perform, he got really excited. Although the guides knew what was going on, they weren't allowed to tell us.

Our guide might have been happy with our position, but we were chosen to dance last. Maybe he had a bet on one of the other countries to win, I thought. Nevertheless, we gave the performance of our lives as a group of dancers. We had to start and finish on the dot of twenty minutes.

We always completed displays like that with a hornpipe, speeding it up at the end, and finishing really fast in a big, long line – just like *Riverdance* years later. And that's how we ended our performance that Sunday night in Dijon to tumultuous applause.

When the results came, I was braced for disappointment because I thought we had finished way down the line.

Then it was announced: 'Irelande sa dor' ... Ireland for gold.

We had won gold for Ireland!

It was an unforgettable moment, one that still gives me a tingle when I think about it today.

* * *

One Sunday night in February 1996, after Ian and I arrived back from our few days at Danny Doherty's school in Coventry, there was a message on my answering machine.

This was pre-mobile phones when the landline was still the king in the world of communication. As I listened to the message, the voice was unmistakeable.

'Hello, is this the Marie Duffy I'm looking for? This is Michael Flatley here. If it is, can you call me back on this number ...'

I never imagined how that call would change the course of the rest of my life.

BIRTH OF A LORD

I was now happily ensconced in Prudhoe, and I loved my life there with Ian.

Prudhoe is a small village in Northumberland, with one of the notable features being a castle which has been there since ancient times when England was at war with Scotland.

The village had a lovely atmosphere, and the people were very friendly and welcoming. You wouldn't go to Prudhoe for the weather, though, because it's cold there most of the time, yet I thought I'd died and gone to heaven when I went to live in that part of the world with Ian.

Ian's house wasn't luxurious, but it was really lovely and very comfortable. One of my passions in life is interior decorating and design; it's something I would have been interested in doing professionally if I'd had the opportunity earlier in life. While I have no training, I have a natural flair for it and I made some suggestions to Ian about changing the interior of the house. Ian was a great DIY man, so we both worked on making alterations and decorating what was now our home together. That was a labour of love for the two of us.

* * *

Ian's invitation at Newcastle Airport to 'go for a pizza sometime' when we first encountered each other still hadn't been fulfilled.

Every now and then, after we married, one of us would say: 'How about going for that pizza?'

It was a joke between us, as we'd talk about that morning when we had first chatted in the airport.

Eventually, though, we did go for a pizza together. The Metro Centre, situated between Gateshead and Newcastle, was at that stage one of the newer shopping malls in Europe. It was very fancy, with nice restaurants and cinemas, and we both loved it.

One afternoon we decided that we'd spend the evening there, finally having our famous pizza with a bottle of wine, and then catching a movie. We got there with lots of time to spare before the movie was due to be screened. We had our pizza and wine, and then we checked our watches and reckoned there was enough time left for another bottle. So we sat and chatted … and finished the second bottle.

We were both now full of the joys of wine as we strolled arm-in-arm into the cinema.

Then I turned to Ian and said, 'All my life I've heard about the back row at the movies. What happens in the back row?'

Ian laughed.

'Well, let's sit in the back row and find out,' he said.

So we sat in the back row. Before the movie had even started we both dropped our heads … and then we snoozed our way through the film from beginning to end.

As we woke up, the credits were rolling.

On the way out we giggled like two teenagers.

'Oh,' I said, 'so that's what happens in the back row at the movies!'

When I reflect on that idyllic period in my life, I realise that I probably didn't really start to live until I met Ian. Up to then, my life had been a constant whirlwind, driven by my commitments to Irish dancing. Ian taught me how to live by just doing ordinary things and enjoying everything you did, even simple things like going for a walk. Like so many people, I hadn't been living in the moment. I wasn't stopping to smell the flowers. I was allowing life to pass me by at a terrifying speed.

Ian taught me how to relax, and it was a blissful period in my life with him. I had never known such happiness.

One of our greatest pleasures was going for a meal to a quaint little local Italian restaurant called Il Piccolo in Prudhoe, run by a handsome Sicilian chef, Manuele Orto, and Pam, his lovely English wife. Pam had met Manuele on a trip abroad when they were both young people, and they had settled in Prudhoe after they got married.

Manuele is a chef extraordinaire, while Pam is also an exceptional person in her role as front of house in the restaurant. She is a very warm, homely lady, whom you instantly feel has been part of your life forever.

When Manuele would finish his work as a chef in the kitchen, he'd then join his customers in the restaurant and entertain everyone with his great

Sicilian sense of humour.

As Ian and I got to know Pam and Manuele, eventually becoming close friends as couples, we learned that they used to refer to us as 'Romeo and Juliet' when we first started going to their restaurant.

'You know who is in tonight?' Pam would say to Manuele.

'Romeo and Juliet?' he'd laugh.

I guess they gave us that name because they saw a happy couple who were very much in love.

* * *

Michael Flatley's message intrigued me when I listened to it on our house phone in Prudhoe after returning from working with Danny Doherty's class in Coventry that Sunday night. I was so curious that I decided to phone him back straight away, despite the late hour.

By now, Michael had left *Riverdance*, in controversial circumstances. As he would later recount in his own autobiography, there was conflict between himself and Moya over his role in the show. Moya Doherty, he said, had raised the money to put *Riverdance* on the road. She regarded him as the star of the show, but also saw him as an employee.

Michael, on the other hand, acknowledged that *Riverdance* could not have happened without Moya. But, because he had created the dance, Michael insisted that *Riverdance* was 'my baby'. The night before the *Riverdance* show was due to open in London for the second time in October 1995, Michael was sacked as negotiations broke down over his contract.

Michael Flatley, of course, was an unstoppable force of nature. Everybody who knew Michael believed that he'd be back. He had too much talent, genius, passion and drive to fade away, despite being dropped by the sensational new dance extravaganza, *Riverdance*.

Sure enough, when I phoned Michael that Sunday night in March 1996, he told me he was putting a new show together. He sounded very upbeat and full of enthusiasm.

'I'm going to Ireland to hold auditions for dancers and I'd like to have a meeting with you,' Michael said.

By coincidence, I was going to be in Dublin for the All-Ireland Champi- onships in Malahide on the north side of the city at that particular time, so we arranged a date and time to get together at an airport hotel.

Ian drove me over to the hotel on a Sunday afternoon and left the two of us alone to talk.

When Michael walked into the room he looked like a guy who had just won the Lottery. He was all fired up with excitement. He told me that after the whole *Riverdance* saga he went off on a trip with some of his close pals and 'got lost for a couple of weeks' to clear his head. That was a good decision, as he returned invigorated and full of ideas for a show that would become *Lord of the Dance*.

'If you are around tomorrow Marie, I'm holding auditions for the show in the Digges Lane Dance Studio here in the city,' he said.

Then he put his hand on mine and added: 'Would you be interested in working on it with me?'

I wasn't expecting that – and my facial expression obviously said as much. 'Would you at least come in and see how it goes?' Michael added with that endearing smile of his. I nodded and said I'd be happy to do that. Michael then relaxed and began asking me about ideas. We talked about a storyline and things that weren't in the other show, *Riverdance*.

As we bounced off each other, I felt we had a very good rapport.

'I'm going back on the late boat tomorrow night,' I added. 'So I can spend the day at the auditions in Digges Lane.'

Michael was very happy with this arrangement, standing up and giving me his familiar warm hug before we went our separate ways.

When I went back to the All-Ireland Championships that afternoon I discovered that a lot of the older dancers were going to the Michael Flatley auditions the following day. There was a buzz of excitement among them as they talked about the auditions and what it might mean.

I overheard the conversations, and then piped up: 'I'll see you at the Michael Flatley auditions tomorrow.'

Heads swivelled in my direction, like I had announced some incredible news story that had just occurred. All eyes were on me.

'You're not going to the auditions, are you?' one dancer eventually exclaimed, breaking the silence.

'Oh yes I am,' I told her, adding: 'I'll see you all there tomorrow.'

Then I strolled away, leaving a troupe of female dancers totally perplexed.

* * *

The Digges Lane Studio was down a side lane not far from Grafton Street, Dublin's upmarket shopping area. I didn't know what to expect as I made my way up that famous thoroughfare on a biting-cold Monday morning. I certainly wasn't prepared for the sight that met my eyes. There was a queue of young men and women that seemed to stretch for miles.

Michael Flatley was equally surprised by the turnout when I met him.

'Wow! Have you seen the line out there, Marie?' he asked.

I nodded.

Derek McKillop, who was right-hand man to Michael's then manager, John Reid, wandered over from a corner of the room. Then we all stood in the middle of the studio looking at each other and wondering where we were going to start. It was a very daunting experience, I have to admit.

Then I snapped out of the moment and quickly got my organising hat on. I had them file into different rooms and line up in an orderly fashion. We set about taking all their names, with poor old Derek being assigned to this task along with other people in the crew.

As the day went on, my excitement and confidence in what we were doing grew and grew because of the quality of the dancers. They were the crème de la crème, world champions or of that standard. I could also see that many of them had very high opinions of themselves, with justification of course. There would be attitude and ego to deal with, I realised.

And I was the one who would be dealing with it.

It would be me telling them what to do.

The first thing that had to be done, of course, was breaking the news to the young hopefuls as to who was staying and who was going home.

'Derek, you'll have to go out and announce the names of the people who are coming back,' I told him, as I just couldn't face the disappointment on the faces of those who didn't get the call back.

Derek looked mortified.

'Thank you for that, Marie,' he said facetiously, as I gave him the list of dancers for the starter group who would be joining Michael Flatley's brand new creation for the world stage. Ian and I then went off on the overnight boat back to England, but by then I had committed to working on Michael's new show, with rehearsals beginning the following Monday.

On Thursday of that week we travelled to Coventry for my classes with Danny's school. When I arrived, there was a message on Danny's phone from Michael Flatley.

Michael told me that they had decided on a music composer for the show. His name was Ronan Hardiman.

I would later learn that Ronan, a small, slim, studious-looking man with round glasses, had been in a rock band during his early career, and had also composed music and jingles for film and TV. He had written the title music for RTÉ television's main evening news, the jingle for top Irish broadcaster Pat Kenny's radio show on RTÉ, as well as a number of commercials for Guinness products and the Irish National Lottery.

Ronan had also done the score for RTÉ's natural history TV series, *Waterways*. He was well known and hugely respected in the worlds of music and media at the time. Later, when I met him, I discovered that Ronan was also great fun with a fabulous sense of humour.

'Maybe you could give Ronan a call, Marie,' Michael added after telling me that he had signed up this talented composer. 'He has come up with some starter bits of music and I'd like you to listen to it and have some ideas on it.'

Michael gave me Ronan's number. I called him from Danny's house, introduced myself and then we had a brief chat about Michael's vision for the show.

Then Ronan said: 'I'd like you to listen to some music that I've composed for the top of the show. If I play it down the phone can you record it?'

I put the phone down and spoke to Danny. He didn't have any recording device in the house. I really needed to have Ronan's music so that I could have some ideas for the choreography when I went back to Dublin on the Monday.

Eventually, we came up with a solution. Ronan would ring Danny's house phone and play his piece of music on the answering machine. Each recording had to be done in a minute.

So that's how it went.

Ronan would call, play his piece of music, which started with gongs. Then he'd call back and do the next piece.

Later that day, I got a recording machine from Danny's class, took it back to his house, and we re-recorded the music on a tape by playing all the phone messages.

From those humble beginnings a worldwide hit show would eventually blossom.

Two of the chosen dancers, Catriona Hale and John Carey, were in Danny's class at that time. They were the first dancers I worked with, and the first to hear the show's music.

'You guys are going over on Monday – listen to this,' I told them.

So I played them the music and spoke about the idea of the gongs and the opening with a group on the floor. That's how it started.

When I went over on Monday morning we had our starter team of dancers, which was about half of the full troupe. This was early March and we were booked to open at The Point in June.

Having taken time out with Ian to smell the roses, I was now back in dancing on a bigger scale than ever.

THE SACRED HEART

I found myself living in Dublin again when rehearsals started for Michael's new show. Ian and I stayed with my brother Seamas and his wife Betty at their home in Hazelbrook Drive, Terenure. We were there for a short time before the company rented an apartment for us.

Every morning, Ian would drive me to work, and then for a period he'd go off exploring the city to pass the day.

One time my sister-in-law Betty asked him: 'What do you do when Marie goes into rehearsals?'

'I go to either the church in Whitefriar Street or Gardiner Street and say some prayers,' Ian replied.

This was a surprise to me, even though I knew that he was quite spiritual. Ian had been baptised, at his own request, in Kansas before we married. It was the church his friends, Ruth and Paul, attended. Later, he started coming to the Catholic Mass with me after we wed.

'I'd like to see what all this kneeling down and standing up is all about,' he explained at the beginning.

One of my favourite Dublin churches to reflect and pray in is Whitefriar Street Church, run by the Carmelite Order. In keeping with their contemplative tradition, it is an oasis of calm and prayerful silence in the midst of a bustling city, and an even busier lifestyle in my case. It's a really beautiful church with all kinds of different altars.

Whitefriar Street Church is also noted for having the relics of St Valentine, which were donated in the nineteenth century by Pope Gregory XVI from their previous location in the cemetery of St Hippolytus in Rome.

It also has the relics of St Albert, a Sicilian who died in 1306. On his feast day, 7 August, a relic of the saint is dipped into the water of St Albert's Well and is said to grant healing of body and mind to those who use the water.

Another Dublin place of worship, peace and tranquility I fell in love with is St Francis Xavier Church, or Gardiner Street Church as it is popularly known.

So, I took Ian along to those churches and they obviously had an impact on him too, particularly the one on Gardiner Street. 'When I drop you off at rehearsals, I go to the church that you took me to on Gardiner Street and I pray to the Sacred Heart,' he told me.

I didn't know why he chose the Sacred Heart. I thought maybe it was the fact that most of the statues in churches are of Jesus with the heart on the outside, representing His divine love for humanity.

When I asked Ian why he prayed to the Sacred Heart, he joked: 'Well, you should always go straight to the top man.' In Kinsealy I had a big statue of the Sacred Heart, which had belonged to my grandmother. It was passed on to my

Aunt Em, who passed it to my mum, who passed it to me.

When I sold my home in Kinsealy and was moving my possessions to Prudhoe, a friend of mine spotted the Sacred Heart statue among the pile and said, 'I'll have Him!'

Ian instantly piped up: 'No, He is coming with us!'

So the Sacred Heart emigrated with me to Prudhoe.

'Where will I put Him?' I said to Ian one day as I was organising my things.

'He should be in our bedroom,' Ian replied.

And that's where He took up residence.

I think Ian found great comfort in religion and, ultimately, in the Catholic Church, despite his run-in with the priest in Kinsealy putting him off it for a time.

There was a Catholic Church called St Agnes's in Crawcrook, the next village to Prudhoe, and he would always come with me to Mass there without being asked. When I discovered the name of the church in Crawcrook I thought it was a good omen.

St Agnes is also the name of my parish church back home in Crumlin, Dublin.

* * *

I was now saying lots of prayers myself as I found myself back in the rat race, and busier than at any other stage of my life. I was also working against a clock that seemed to be ticking down time faster than it should, as we prepared for the opening night of Michael Flatley's new show.

It was the deadline, rather than the actual staging of the show, that gave me sleepless nights. The show was no hardship to me because all my past experience then came into play. It was then I appreciated what I had learned when I was putting on shows in the Dublin national schools, and on the road at festivals around Europe with Inis Ealga. Now I was using all those skills in my new role with Michael Flatley.

The show was created in different ways. Sometimes Michael put rhythms together and we'd show them to Ronan and say, 'Will you put a tune to that?' Other times Ronan would send us music and we'd put steps to it.

For a short time before we got apartments, we were staying at the luxurious Westbury Hotel off Grafton Street. One day, the phone rang while I was taking a shower and Ian answered it.

'Ronan has some new music for you to listen to,' Ian said, popping his head into the bathroom.

I quickly dried off and raced to the phone in the bedroom. Ronan then played me a piece of music that would turn out to be 'Breakout', or 'strip jig', which was our pet name for it because it's the dance scene where the girls whip off their skirts in the show. It was an appropriate piece of music at that moment given my state of undress.

'Is this time alright for you for this number?' Ronan asked.

'Hold on,' I said as I started dancing to the music in my birthday suit.

'Up a bit,' I said, as I took some steps.

'Okay, down a bit.'

'A bit faster.'

'Now slower.'

Ian was doubled over with laughter in the corner of the room.

I was just glad for Ronan's sake that we weren't on Skype.

* * *

Michael brought Irish dancing several steps down the line in *Riverdance*, but he took it into the stratosphere in movements, sexiness and costumes with *Lord of the Dance*. However, it took a lot of blood, sweat and tears to create that vision.

It was Michael and dance captain Daire Nolan who put the guys through their paces every day, while I trained the girls. But I would have both the guys and girls in from early morning for rehearsals and, of course, 'the Marie Duffy exercises'.

At first, there was resistance from the big, tough young men who had been dancing all their lives in competition without a warm-up regime.

Their attitude was: 'You want us to do this girlie stuff, like stretching!'

It took a lot of persuasion on my part to get them into that mindset. I pointed out to them that every other form of dance at the highest level had those exercises at its core. Eventually, they did listen when their bodies started to rebel.

This was dancing on a scale that they had never experienced before. It was totally different to competitive dancing. They had to retrain in so many ways. From being still and stiff with arms down by their sides in Irish dancing, they now had the challenge of expressing themselves in all kinds of ways, both physically and emotionally. They were now using their bodies, their arms, their expressions, as well as dancing. It was a totally new discipline.

Soon they were all struggling with aches and pains and sore muscles. And pain is a great way to get attention. They then saw the importance and the benefit of 'the Marie Duffy exercises'.

We had a very good team: Daire Nolan as mentioned was the male captain, while Catriona Hale filled that role among the females. We were still trying out different leads, with top dancers like Bernadette Flynn, Gillian Norris and

Areleen Ní Bhaoil. One day Michael would like one, the next day he would prefer the other.

Michael kept the storyline of the show simple. It was the age-old tale of good versus evil; the bad guy and the good guy; the temptress and the good girl. Because we were starting from scratch we took it number by number, with whatever piece of music Ronan had ready.

Ronan had his own way of composing music, so it took us both a while to find a common language to marry the music and the dances.

It was an inspired move by Michael to hire Ronan, who was then a new kid on the block. He created his own style in his own way and put his stamp musically on *Lord of the Dance*.

Michael was the creative genius who would paint a picture of what he wanted, and Ronan would go off and talk to myself and the dance captain, Daire, as he tried to figure it all out. Then we would tweak it in the dance studio, working together as a whole team.

We became a tight little unit.

In the daily routine, I worked with the dancers in the morning and then Michael would come in and work with us in the afternoon and we'd finish around six in the evening.

There was a very lively entertainment venue called Break for the Border next door to the Digges Lane Studio, and it obviously had some kind of a magnet that occasionally pulled in our dancers. With Michael's zest for life, of course he was the ringleader. He was all for young people having a good time. However, occasionally they had too much of a good time for my liking, particularly with a heart-stopping deadline on the horizon.

One particular morning I arrived into the studio to find that all the dancers had turned into Martians. At least that's how they looked to me – they were all green in the face. Inside I was fuming when I saw the state of them. I had warned them so many times about not overdoing their partying when they had downtime because there was so much work to do in a very short period of time.

At first, I considered sending them all home in disgrace that morning. Then I had a better idea. I thought, well, you don't listen, so now you got to learn by paying the price. And I put them through their paces ten times harder over the next few hours.

It was around noon when Derek McKillop popped in to see how things were going. He had obviously peeped in and felt that everything was fine and dandy. Judging by the smile on his face, he had no idea that a torrent of abuse was about to be unleashed on him – by me!

'Look at the state of the people in this room!' I said, summoning up my inner witch from hell.

Derek suddenly looked very sheepish. He stood and listened to my rant for a couple of minutes before exiting the studio when I ran out of steam.

I later learned that he went straight to a phone and called Michael to warn him.

'You had better not come in here today; I have just been stripped down to short pants,' he told him.

An hour later, I see Michael's head peeping around the door like a bold child, with that big grin on his face that is so disarming. I gave him a dirty look, shook my head at him ... and then burst out laughing.

On reflection, I realised that it was important for the dancers to let off steam every now and then to keep up their enthusiasm and their spirit. I had them on a very strict cycle of dancing and rehearsing. I was probably a very hard taskmaster, but I had to be because opening night was coming up very fast. It was a scary deadline. So it was hard going and hard work. Every day we would be doing a new piece, adding something extra to the show, and there were thirty-six dancers to keep in shape.

* * *

By now, the dance troupe were starting to bond together as people. Apart from the discipline of the show rehearsals, the young guys and girls, ranging in age from sixteen to twenty, were also coming to terms with a new life in a strange environment. Many of them were living away from home for the first time, so I am sure they were having to cope with homesickness and all kinds of emotions. I found myself being a mother to them as well.

Until the show opened we didn't have catering, so they were each given a daily allowance to cover their expenses, including their food. Their accommodation in houses and apartments had been taken care of, but we had to drill into them the importance of keeping the rental properties clean and damage-free. Teenagers can be very messy, so there were strict rules about being tidy. There were a few scary parties at the beginning, but they were knocked on the head pretty fast. It was just the normal kind of stuff that you would expect from teenagers, but we had to ensure that things never got out of hand. And, of course, we lectured them on the importance of having respect for their neighbours and keeping the noise down. Mind you, I had my own embarrassing experience with the neighbours during that period. Some of the lads were staying in a rented house in the Clonskeagh area of south Dublin, and a fancy dress party had been organised to celebrate one of their birthdays. Although I had been invited, I decided not to go as it came at the end of a long working day for me. However, one of the girls insisted that I accompany her, so I eventually gave in after some arm-twisting.

I was wearing dark pants and a dark top, and the girl who was taking me along with her had a brainwave that I should put a black stocking over my head and go to the fancy dress shindig as the 'surprise dance star who is going to be unveiled for the show'.

The two of us hopped in a taxi from the city centre out to Clonskeagh, eventually reaching the address for the party. Before ringing the doorbell I put the black stocking over my head. There was no answer, so we knocked a couple of times until eventually the door was opened – by an elderly couple!

You can imagine the look of shock, horror and fright on their faces when they saw this menacing figure standing there on their doorstep dressed in black and wearing a balaclava.

Next the screeching started, and I'm sure you could hear the screams of the poor old lady all across the city.

Well, the two of us immediately turned on our heels and took off like a shot with our tails between our legs.

We eventually found the right house, where the party was in full swing, several doors down the street.

And, needless to say, I was the joke of the night.

While some of the young dancers may have been struggling to come to terms with life out in the big, bad world on their own for the first time, this was also an exciting period in their young lives.

For most of them, it was their first taste of freedom and, with the mix of boys and girls, inevitably there were a lot of first romances. We noticed a lot of couples forming, and the majority of them stuck together, which was good for stability in the troupe.

Later, we would have many, many marriages.

ON THE ROAD

TO THE OSCARS

The Point Theatre, Ireland's biggest concert arena located in the docklands area of Dublin city, was the setting for the launch of *Lord of the Dance* on Friday, 28 June 1996, with the premiere planned for the following Tuesday, 2 July.

I will always remember the shock and awe I experienced walking in to the Point, which is now the fabulous 3Arena, and seeing the show's set for the first time. It was gigantic, fantastic, and thrilling.

I'd never imagined being involved with a production on that scale, so looking at the stage, which seemed to be the size of a football pitch, gave my heart a little jump. A shiver went down my spine, but it was sparked by excitement rather than fear because I felt that we were prepared for the challenge to come. There were some small finishing touches to be completed here and there on a couple of the numbers, but nothing of major concern.

After months of frantic activity and hard graft, the dance troupe was now like an elite army about to go into battle. All the young people were well practised and drilled, with their entrances and exits perfected. They were very tight, so their confidence was really high. They were fit, ready and raring to go. And I just couldn't wait to see them up and running.

Watching the crowd file into the Point that night brought more excitement. Thousands had come to see the new Michael Flatley extravaganza that had been built up in the local media by Irish publicist Chris Roche, a gentle giant of a man. Michael's dream of taking it into major arenas around the world didn't look so far-fetched at that moment.

Backstage, I listened as Michael gave the dancers a final pep talk before the curtain went up. He was trying to calm them down, reassure them that they were the best dancers in the world, and send them out on stage with that kind of self-belief.

Then I went out and took my seat in front of the stage beside Arlene Phillips, a major figure in the world of dance who was a director on the show alongside Michael.

Arlene was a household name in Britain as the former director and choreographer of Hot Gossip, a dance troupe she had formed in 1974. They were regularly featured on *The Kenny Everett Show*, and they even had a hit in the UK charts, backing Sarah Brightman on 'I Lost My Heart To A Starship Trooper'. Arlene had also worked in London's West End and around the world as a director and choreographer on major shows; later she would star as a judge on *Strictly Come Dancing*.

It was Michael's then manager, John Reid, who had brought Arlene on board for *Lord of the Dance*.

Harvey Goldsmith was our promoter and he was in the major league, having run concerts for superstar acts like Led Zeppelin, Elton John, Queen, U2 and Madonna.

Watching *Lord of the Dance* come to life before our eyes in the Point that night is a piece of magic that will never leave my mind. That's the show I'll always remember, seeing it for the first time with the applause of the Irish audience ringing in my ears.

As the night went on, and I relaxed as I saw how smoothly the performance was running, a wave of emotion swept over me.

My mind drifted back to my mother, and I was wishing for her to be there beside me to see this wonderful show that her daughter *Mar*-ee was now working on. This was where her vision, and the money she spent on me, had taken me. She had been determined to give me every opportunity in life to be the person I became.

I remember thinking several times during the performance: 'I wish Mum could be here now to see this.'

When the show reached its climax with that big number that sounds like a million feet dancing at the speed of light, the audience tore the place down. They sprung to their feet whooping, hollering, whistling and clapping wildly as if their lives depended on it.

Michael Flatley's smile was as wide as the gigantic stage that night.

Lord of the Dance, his creation, had been a spectacular hit.

* * *

A few nights later we gathered around a television in the green room at the Point. The female dancers were jumping up and down with glee, while the guys pretended to be cool, even though it was quite obvious that they were bursting with excitement as they watched a *Lord of the Dance* opening night report on the RTÉ TV early evening news.

There were shots of the crowd arriving at the Point for the show, and then it went to a recording of the dancers inside the venue.

'Hey, it's us!' The girls were now bouncing around the room with excitement.

Michael and I glanced at each other, and judging by the gleam in his eyes I knew that he felt he'd died and gone to heaven.

With several performances under their belt, the dancers were comfortable and confident as they went out on stage for their big official opening night. I took my seat out front, passing our Irish promoter, a lovely old-school gentleman called Jim Aiken, in the wings. Jim, who had created the template for Ireland's concert scene as the first promoter to bring in major international music stars on tour, looked really pleased with the way the public were responding to the show.

Waiting for the opening number my emotions were a mixture of nerves and excitement. There is always the niggling worry that something will go wrong. No matter how well you prepare, there's the danger of an unexpected event happening. You always worry about a fall or an injury and the domino effect that would set off. But from the very start I could see that the dancers were supremely confident.

They were also buzzing with excitement, and, as it turned out, the show went smoothly with no glitches.

On opening night it struck me that while Michael Flatley's fantastic charm and charisma had a major part to play in the success of *Lord of the Dance*, the energy and enthusiasm of the dancers, and the joy they exuded, were also infectious. That's also the magic that pulled in the audience, got them involved in the show and ultimately had them jumping out of their seats.

I've always said that to dancers: 'The night you become complacent and don't get the audience out of their seats is the time you start to worry.'

But there were no worries that night.

* * *

Lord of the Dance was now a sensation.

After Dublin, the world beckoned.

First stop was Liverpool in England, where the warmth of the reception the show received matched Dublin. It was the same in Manchester. But Michael suffered a serious injury in Manchester when he tore his calf muscle during the first half of the show.

This caused major backstage drama.

Michael struggled through to the end of the first half, but our then production manager Martin Flitton came to me and said he would not be able to go back on when the show resumed

Michael's understudy John Carey had been trained for this moment during rehearsals, but it was still a shock for him to be told that he was going to have to take over the role.

It was a shock for me as well.

The audience were then informed that Michael had sustained an injury and could not return to the stage. Meanwhile, I took John aside and we briefly ran through the second half parts with the leading lady and the opposite male lead, the bad guy.

As the curtain came up for the second half, I held my breath. I had total confidence in John's ability, but in a live show anything can happen.

As it transpired, John gave the performance of his life, completing the show without a hitch. And at the end he received tumultuous applause from the audience who appreciated the task he had taken on, and the success he had made of it.

The injury should have put Michael Flatley out of action for a long time, possibly a year, but there was a sold-out run at The Coliseum in London coming up, including a Royal Command Performance for Prince Charles.

I have no idea how he managed it, but with expert help from our dance therapist and reiki healer Derry Ann Morgan, along with the power of positive thinking, and an incredible ability to battle through horrendous pain, Michael got back up on stage four days later.

It was truly a miracle.

No one could believe it. He was like a gladiator. As Prince Charles sat back and enjoyed the star performance of Michael Flatley that night, he had no idea of the superhuman effort it had taken to pull off that dazzling dance display.

We had been booked into London's Coliseum for a week, but such was the phenomenal demand for tickets that we ended up playing sold-out shows there for an entire month.

Michael's dream to take *Lord of the Dance* around the globe then proceeded with Australia, where the crowds went crazy. They absolutely loved it. The whole of the Irish dancing world in Oz came out to see it.

Ian was with me on the tour, so this was a very exciting time in our lives. It was a new chapter and new experiences that we never envisaged when we got together and married. We were travelling around the world with a hit show and it couldn't have been a better life at that time.

However, there was a worrying couple of days when Ian took a bit of a turn in Australia and felt unwell. Like many men, he refused to go to a doctor at the time, despite my insistence. Then he seemed fine, so I let it go after he promised to have a medical check when we got home.

It was in Australia that I celebrated my fiftieth birthday, in a place called Newcastle, by a strange coincidence. Martin Flitton organised a surprise party for me, and Michael ordered a fantastic cake that I still remember to this day. I had the best night, with Ian by my side. I had to pinch myself that night, remembering where I was and what I was doing at the age of fifty!

* * *

There was often more drama off the stage than on it when we were out on the road with *Lord of the Dance*.

When London's Wembley Arena appeared on our tour schedule for 1997 there was huge excitement among the troupe. It is one of those iconic venues in the world of live entertainment. For performers, playing Wembley Arena is a true mark of success. Michael Flatley was just thrilled when the shows started selling out at the venue; and they went on to break records, with twenty-two successive nights.

In the build-up to the opening night, Michael had no idea that there was a major saga unfolding in the troupe. One of our dancers, Jimmy Murrihy, had been deported from the UK and sent back home to the States, giving me a major headache to sort out.

Jimmy, who was raised in Boston by Irish parents, had gone home to spend Christmas with his family. When he was returning a few days later, Jimmy was stopped by customs at Heathrow Airport and refused entry.

It transpired that there was an issue with his visa documentation.

A customs officer contacted the *Lord of the Dance* company manager to inform him. After lots of pleading from our side, Jimmy was allowed into the country for twenty-four hours while customs decided what to do with him. *Lord of the Dance* was then in Newcastle, with the next stop Wembley Arena.

Unfortunately for Jimmy, his next stop was going to be Boston. The word came back that he was being deported, and so the following day Jimmy flew from Newcastle to Heathrow Airport, where he was held under armed guard until it was time for him to board the plane. Jimmy remembers feeling like a major criminal at the time, particularly after he was informed that his bags wouldn't be put on the plane until he had boarded.

Jimmy's American passport was then stamped: DEPORTED.

Naturally, Jimmy was devastated, as it had also been his dream to perform at Wembley Arena. So, along with the *Lord of the Dance* management, I then set in motion my mission: 'How to get a Yank an Irish passport in twenty-four hours.'

Fortunately, as Jimmy's parents were originally from Ireland and had their births and marriage certs in their possession, they met their son at Boston airport with all the required documentation.

At 7 p.m. that evening we got Jimmy back out of Boston – and his next destination was Ireland. Jimmy arrived in to Dublin airport at 6 a.m. the following morning. As luck would have it, I had a friend working in the Dublin Passport Office, so Jimmy was waiting outside the door when the office opened that morning, and shortly afterwards he had an emergency Irish passport in his hand. By lunchtime, we had Jimmy on a flight from Dublin to London's Heathrow Airport where the whole shenanigans had started a couple of days earlier. This time he had no problem getting through on his Irish passport.

Jimmy Murrihy arrived at Wembley Arena that evening for the opening night of *Lord of the Dance* with just an hour to spare.

And he gave the performance of his life.

Michael Flatley had been blissfully unaware of the drama that was unfolding behind the scenes as he was doing his round of media interviews and getting ready for the performance in the build-up to that big night at Wembley.

We felt that he had enough on his mind without having to worry about one of his dancers getting the boot out of Britain.

When told later, Michael saw the funny side of the incident and gave Jimmy a good-natured slagging.

Jimmy tells me that he kept his old passport as a souvenir of the day he was deported from the UK.

* * *

The big prize for Michael would be success in America with *Lord of the Dance*. Most hugely ambitious and driven people in show business dream of cracking America, and Michael was no different. The difference with Michael is that he doesn't just dream, he makes it happen.

One of the most exciting aspects of working with Michael Flatley was feeding off his positivity. He is a super-positive person.

So, when Michael said, 'We're going to take this show to the Oscars,' I believed him.

If we got the opportunity to perform at the Oscars in Los Angeles, it would put *Lord of the Dance* on the map in America and around the globe. It's the biggest night of the year in show business, so pitching to get his show on to the stage at the 1997 Academy Awards was an inspired move. It has a worldwide audience of more than one billion people!

'We got it, Marie. We got the Oscars!' Michael told me one day.

By the look on his face, you'd think he had hit the jackpot and cleaned out all the casinos in Las Vegas.

'Marie, what did I tell you? We're going to put Irish dancing on the biggest stage in the world,' he said, giving me a huge hug.

Is there anyone out there who had doubted him? Well, maybe a few. But they hadn't factored in Michael's power of positive thinking, enormous charm, charisma, stage wizardry and fearlessness.

But ultimately it was his simple decision to just ask for *Lord of the Dance* to be considered as a performance act for the Oscars.

If you don't ask, you don't receive, as they say.

All they can say is no.

So Michael asked.

And now we were going to be performing at the Oscars in Hollywood!

Before that special night, *Lord of the Dance* already had an American tour in place. And off we went playing Michael's home town of Chicago, as well as Minneapolis, Boston and Philadelphia.

The tour included a series of shows at the iconic and historic Radio City theatre in New York that March, 1997. To be a hot ticket in New York was really special. To be performing in Radio City on St Patrick's Night was the icing on the cake.

The Irish took over the town that night. Relatives of the cast – mothers, fathers, brothers, sisters, aunts, uncles, cousins and distant cousins – flew in from all over Ireland and the UK for the occasion. There was great pride in the show, and the excitement was at fever pitch.

My husband Ian was so proud of me being involved in this wonderful extravaganza that was now creating such a buzz in New York of all places.

He said to me in the lead up to it, 'How about asking Barry and Kim and young Ian to come over for the show?'

I thought it would be so lovely to have Ian's son Barry, his wife, Kim, and their son, Ian Jnr, with us during that special time in New York. I really loved Barry, although our relationship had been strained when Ian and I first got together. Barry had been very close to his mother, Iris. Then I turned up in his father's life just a short time after she had died. I completely understood why he initially had a problem coming to terms with his dad's new relationship. Barry needed time to grieve before he could begin to accept me being Ian's new partner.

And that's how it went.

Time gradually sorted it out.

Barry and Kim were delighted with the offer to join us in New York with young Ian, so we booked their flights and hotel. Ian was a great shopper, which was unusual for a man. So when they arrived, he was like a kid taking Barry, Kim and Ian Jnr sightseeing and shopping in the 'Big Apple'.

Then St Patrick's Day came around and it was a frantic day. I went through rehearsals with the dancers, and then I rushed back to the hotel to change. Before leaving for the show, I gave Ian the invites to the after-party for our families, friends, cast members, parents and dance teachers who were there for the event.

The show was flying success-wise at this stage, and I had dance teachers from all over America coming to see it, and looking for tickets to the after-show party. It was going to be the Irish party of the year in New York.

One of the teachers on the west coast of America hadn't confirmed that she was coming, so there were no tickets for her. Martin Flitton came in and said to me: 'You are in trouble. There's a lady in the office and you don't have a ticket for her.'

She had booked her flight and hotel, but didn't realise she hadn't confirmed her attendance at the show. I then gave her my ticket and a pass for the after-show party.

There were so many loose ends to tie up before the show opened, and I got caught up in all of that work. Then Ian came to escort me down to the show, but when we strolled up to a security check they wouldn't let me through because I had no ticket and no pass.

Ian was horrified. 'Do you know who this is? This is my wife, she works on this show,' he declared to an unimpressed young security guard.

As well as the anger, I could see the pride in Ian's face at that moment. I knew that he was as proud as punch of me.

Fortunately, Martin Flitton appeared on the scene by chance and sorted out the problem. Then we took our seats, sat back and enjoyed every moment of the performance, just like the rest of the auditorium.

Everyone in the show was on fire that night, and it was such a great atmosphere with so many family members, friends and associates from all walks of life in the audience.

One of the dancers, Catriona Hale, had a heart-stopping moment when velcro on the stage curtains caught her costume and she struggled in vain to hang on to her spot on the stage as the curtains were pulled away.

Michael said that ever since he was a kid he'd dreamt of performing at Radio City. To be by his side that night and to share the moment as he realised his dream was such a privilege.

The only event that could top that experience was the Oscars.

* * *

After a week of shows in Radio City, next stop was Hollywood, California, where we would live the dream for a couple of weeks.

If you're in show business, then Hollywood is the stuff of fantasies. And it's an unbelievable, 'pinch yourself' moment when you end up in 'Tinseltown'. Nothing can prepare you for the excitement you experience.

But here we all were, rolling into town for a star performance on the biggest showbiz night in the world. Michael Flatley had made that happen for all of us, and, in turn, everyone in the troupe had helped him to achieve his ultimate goal through our talent, dedication and sheer hard work.

We arrived a week before the Oscars to settle in and rehearse for the *Lord of the Dance* showpiece. If we needed any reminding that we were now in the superstar league, then all we had to do was take a look at the other two acts on the bill that night.

We were the entertainers, along with Madonna and Celine Dion. So no pressure at all then!

There were about forty of us in *Lord of the Dance* and we were all staying in a lovely hotel in Beverly Hills. Our dancers ranged in age from sixteen to their early twenties, so you can imagine how thrilling it was for them to be living in Beverly Hills. This was straight out of the movies for them.

We had hired a studio, and the mornings were dedicated to rehearsing for our performance. I would take them to the studio and we'd rehearse, rehearse, rehearse. The dancers were in top shape, but we weren't taking anything for granted. We wanted them to be razor sharp for this showcase performance from *Lord of the Dance*.

The Oscars was the show's shop window for America and around the world, and the dancers had to give the performance of their lives.

There had to be a good balance in their daily routine, of course. If you put in too much work there is always the danger of burnout. So they all had the afternoons free to go and experience Los Angeles, which is what they did.

Open-top cars were hired by the guys to cruise along the coast, stopping to take it all in. There was shopping, or at least window shopping, to be experienced on Rodeo Drive. They had seen it all in the movies; now they had the opportunity to soak up all this American culture.

The week flew by, and finally the big day arrived. We were up at the crack of dawn as we had a full day of rehearsals at Shrine Auditorium, which was the venue for the Oscars. A large coach sat purring on the forecourt outside our Beverly Hills hotel, and as we all filed on the atmosphere inside was electric with excitement and nerves. On the journey to the auditorium it was like being in a beehive with the buzz of conversation between the dancers.

They were like children going to meet Santa Claus.

When we arrived, a team of security was waiting to escort us off the coach, take us up the famous red carpet and into the auditorium. Everywhere we went that week there were life-size Oscars as the town got into the party spirit.

The dancers were already in the 'zone', but it really became a reality when we entered the venue. On our way to the dressing rooms we spotted life-size cardboard cut-outs of the stars in the seats where they would be sitting during the awards show later that night. The pictures were there for the rehearsals, so that the camera crews would know where to pick out the stars when their names were called.

The dancers were beside themselves with excitement even before they clapped eyes on the famous actors and actresses in person. During the first rehearsals, I could hear squeals of: 'Oooh! Look who I'm dancing in front of!'

Another screeched: 'Oh my god, look who is in my direct eyeline!'

Movies like *The English Patient*, *The People vs. Larry Flynt*, *Jerry Maguire*,

Independence Day, Evita, Shine, Michael Collins and *Fargo* were up for Oscars that night.

We were looking at cut-outs of stars that included Ralph Fiennes, Woody Harrelson, Tom Cruise, Diane Keaton, Emily Watson and Juliette Binoche in the audience.

It was going to be an incredible experience for the dancers performing in front of Hollywood royalty, and in rehearsals it took me a while to get them settled and focused on the dance number. But eventually their professionalism kicked in, and by the final rehearsal Michael's beaming face told them that they were in great shape for what lay ahead.

Ian and I went back to the hotel to get dressed up in our evening wear. I wore a long black dress and jacket, while Ian looked really dashing in black tie. Then it was back to Shrine Auditorium and a trip up the red carpet, just a couple of hours before all the movie stars would take a stroll behind the same velvet rope, stopping to give endless sound bites to the assembled media.

The glamour, glitz and style at the Oscars is overwhelming. Every hair-dresser and make-up artist in Hollywood makes a fortune when that show comes to town. Everywhere I looked inside the auditorium there were shards of light shooting from chandeliers, and then came the parade of actresses and other major personalities in fabulous dresses. This was fashion heaven for the ladies.

It is just the most fantastic day and night in show business.

Backstage, our dancers finally got to rub shoulders with stars in the flesh as the countdown began to the opening. They were bumping into them in dressing rooms and corridors and all corners of the auditorium. Souvenir photographs were snapped with the icons, and autographs were secured. Then we were brought to a holding area before our performance and the dancers had their eyes out on sticks as they spotted lots more A-list celebrities wandering through.

'Oh my God, did you see who just passed by!' a dancer said, unable to contain her excitement as Tom Cruise disappeared down the line

A lifetime of memories were banked that day.

Then came the performance, and my nerves shot through the roof. But within seconds they were replaced by an overwhelming sense of pride. The dancers were just fabulous and faultless.

There was a heart-stopping moment when Michael tore across the stage and was nearly sent flying to the floor by a cameraman with a hand-held camera who appeared out of nowhere. Later we learned that the camera operator hadn't been at the dress rehearsal, so he didn't realise that Michael would be shooting across the stage at a hundred miles an hour. He was going at a ferocious speed – the cameraman couldn't get out of the way – but in a split second Michael shot around him without stumbling or missing a beat and thus avoided a disastrous collision. Michael, being the pro that he is, made it look so seamless that nobody noticed anything unusual about it.

At the end, the reception and the applause that the *Lord of the Dance* performance received was incredible.

We had done it. We had gone to the Oscars with a new show, and we'd come away with, as Michael would tell us, 'the greatest show on earth'.

Michael Flatley's *Lord of the Dance* was now a phenomenon in its own right.

As Michael went off to a reception, I joined the dancers for a meal out with lots of drinks to toast the experience of a lifetime.

I remember thinking in the middle of the hooley that night: 'It's amazing where Irish dancing and the one, two, threes can take you.'

All the way to the Oscars.

Lord of the Dance was then booked in for more shows at a local theatre, but in the meantime we had a couple of days off to relax in Los Angeles. Ian loved driving, so he was keen to get out on the highways. We rented a car, put the roof down, and off we went rolling along the freeway.

We stopped off in Malibu and Ian phoned his son, Barry, who had returned to the UK after his trip to New York.

'This is great, son, it is fabulous,' Ian told Barry.

He was on top of the world at that moment, apart from a bit of a cold that he was trying to shake off. We said we would get some pills to sort that out.

Neither Ian nor myself had any inkling of what awaited us around the corner.

HELL ON EARTH

After our thrilling night at the Oscars, *Lord of the Dance* moved into the Universal Amphitheatre in Los Angeles for a short run of shows.

Ian's cold got worse, so he stayed behind at our hotel on the first day as he tried to shake it off. The next night he felt well enough to come to the show. Matt Meleady's daughter, Doireann, lives in California. Doireann was away, but her husband, John Hoy, came to see the performance that night. Afterwards, Ian and I joined John for a drink before we walked back to our hotel.

When we retired to bed, Ian was in good form. His cold had improved and he had no complaints or pains, or if he did he didn't mention them. Around five in the morning I came out of a deep sleep and it took me a few seconds to get my bearings.

Then I heard Ian's voice. 'Your arm is heavy, can you lift it,' he said quietly.

I'd had my arm around his chest.

So I moved it, but then as I became more alert I noticed that Ian had gone very still.

I called his name and he didn't answer.

Then I jumped up in the bed with fright. I instinctively checked his wrist for a pulse, but I couldn't get one. In panic, I then felt his neck for one, and it was beating very fast.

My own heart was now racing with absolute fear as I frantically dialled reception to raise the alarm. The hotel receptionist said she'd get the paramedics up immediately.

As I waited for what seemed like an eternity, but in reality was just minutes, Ian started to come round.

He was dazed.

'What's the matter?' Ian asked.

'You just passed out,' I told him.

'I had this pain,' he said, still looking quite disorientated.

'Don't worry, I've called the paramedics,' I assured him.

'Oh, I'm fine now,' he protested, getting up and out of bed.

I jumped out and immediately got him to sit down on a chair. He kept saying he didn't want the paramedics. But very quickly there was a knock on the door and they came in.

'I'm okay now, I'm fine,' he insisted to them.

I was adamant that they should check him out, so he relented. They discovered that his pulse was still very high and they said Ian needed to go to hospital. He didn't want to go, but we persuaded him, saying it would only be a couple of hours.

The medics wanted to take Ian out to the ambulance on a stretcher, but he was having none of it.

'I'm feeling fine. I can walk,' he told them.

Eventually he compromised, agreeing to be wheeled out in a chair. I left a message on one of the *Lord of the Dance* company phones telling them what had happened and where I could be located.

In the ambulance the medics plugged Ian in to lots of equipment and did their best to keep him calm as we raced to the emergency department of St Joseph's Hospital in Beverly Hills.

Within a short time Ian was in a bed in a little unit. He was sitting up, talking normally and in great form. The doctor was trying to get him to stay quiet, but Ian was insisting on telling him all about *Lord of the Dance* and the important role that I was playing in the show that was now running in Hollywood.

Then the doctor said, 'Just relax, I am going to give you some medication.'

I was sitting in a chair in the little unit at the time. They gave him the medication and within seconds alarms were going off. Even to this day I can still hear those alarms in my head. They never leave you.

Nurses took me by the arm and rushed me out to a room where I was left on my own. I felt ill with fright and worry as I feared the worst. There was no one to consult or talk to. It would still be a couple of hours before anyone from *Lord of the Dance* woke up and got my message.

So I sat there on my own, praying hard to the Sacred Heart.

Eventually a doctor came in and broke the news that Ian had suffered cardiac arrest.

'He lost oxygen for twenty minutes, so we don't know the effects of that,' the doctor added.

The first people to arrive from *Lord of the Dance* that morning were manager Martin Flitton and physiotherapist Derry Ann Morgan. They stayed with me for most of the day. We sat by Ian's bed and there wasn't a movement or a sound or a sign of life out of him. I was just devastated, and so was everyone in the company when the news filtered through to them.

I heard later that the dancers were all phoning their parents back home to tell them that something terrible had happened to Ian. By that time, Ian was well known to everyone in the Irish dancing world, so they were all shocked.

* * *

The days slipped by, *Lord of the Dance* moved on as the tour continued around America, but the company kept on my accommodation at the hotel. Going back to our hotel for a rest during the first couple of days was the most awful experience. I couldn't stay in the same room where Ian had taken ill, so they moved me to a different one, although the size, layout and interior décor was exactly the same.

When I closed the door and was left on my own I could see every second of Ian's attack and the arrival of the medics being played out over and over.

It was like some horrible nightmare, except it was real.

Barry later arrived over from Scotland and we had a very emotional reunion. It was all so different from his joyful experience with Ian in New York just a couple of weeks earlier. Back then, we were all on top of the world and having the time of our lives.

It's frightening to think how lovely lives can be ripped apart in seconds.

Barry was devastated seeing his father lying lifeless in a hospital bed, all wired up and attached to a life-support machine. Barry stayed for a few days, but then he had to return home for his work. I was praying so hard to the Sacred Heart to spare Ian and to bring him back to me. A week went by and there was no improvement in Ian's condition.

At this point the neurosurgeons were talking to me about switching off the life-support machine because there was no response from him. I didn't entertain that at all. I told them that in the world where I was brought up, we believed that where there is life there is hope. I begged them to do everything in their power to resuscitate Ian.

The hospital staff were very good. I would go in at 8 a.m. every day and stay until 11 p.m. I refused to give up on Ian without a fight. While I was sitting in the unit day in and day out I would continually talk to Ian because I believed that he could hear me even though there was no response from him.

And I prayed and prayed.

My prayers to the Sacred Heart were answered when, after a couple of weeks, Ian suddenly opened his eyes one day. No one could believe it. It was like a little miracle – but I had never given up hope. I was sitting by his bed at the time, and as he came around I could see that after some time he recognised me.

However, the heart attack had done a lot of damage. Ian was now paralysed and unable to speak. I was told that he would never walk again.

Now that Ian had recovered consciousness, I was under no illusion about the future. I knew that we now faced a long road to get Ian a decent quality of life again. I was going to be spending months in Hollywood at St Joseph's Hospital. Unicorn Entertainment, the company Michael set up to run *Lord of the Dance*, was very supportive. They organised an apartment for me to live in while I was in Hollywood.

Leaving the hotel and all the horrible memories that it brought up again and again was such a relief.

In times of need and trouble, as I knew by then after losing my mother, the Irish dancing community rally round you.

Doireann Ní Mhaoiléidigh and her husband John lived at least two hours away from the hospital. But they came to be with me every day, only leaving to do their dance classes, and then coming back to me. Their support was way beyond the call of duty.

Margaret Cleary, another dance teacher in Los Angeles, was a tremendous friend who made regular visits. Katie, her daughter, was only a child at the time, and she would bring her on the visits. As time went on, Katie struck up a bond with Ian.

Later, Margaret introduced me to Mary Fox, whom she knew through her class. Mary became my guardian angel, visiting me day and night.

* * *

Ian's therapy was a torture for the poor man, and my heart was torn as we put him through his hell. Trying to teach him to read and speak again wasn't easy because he was a very proud man and I'm sure he felt that he was being tutored like a child. In effect, that's exactly how he was being treated because he was learning how to speak all over again.

But, as painful as it was for all of us, we never gave up. We knew it was worth trying as we saw some good signs in Ian.

If you asked Ian, 'Where is the glass?', he would point to it.

So, we knew that his brain was functioning to a degree.

However, if you asked him, 'What is it called?', he couldn't find the word for it.

Then he would get very frustrated with himself, and with us.

The occupational therapists were very good and very patient. I watched intently and learnt from them so that I could continue what they were doing.

I did learn a lot from them.

One day I overheard a neurosurgeon saying to staff, 'Watch the way she handles him, you can learn from her.'

But it broke my heart to see the pain in Ian's face as he struggled to express himself. It wasn't the state that Ian, or any of us, would want in life.

There were times when I got very cross with God. I would ask over and over why, after waiting a lifetime for Ian to come into my life, had I only been given five years with him. But then I would reflect and accept that we'd had five lovely years before his heart attack. You look at some people who are a lifetime together and they don't even have five good years. They have years of hell. We'd had a fantastic five years, so that was a gift.

It was no hardship for me to spend all day, every day looking after Ian. I would help to get him in and out of bed, wash and dress him. I cut his hair, washed and dried it. I kept him as smart as he always liked to be before his devastating heart attack. I wanted to look after his every need, his every want. And it wasn't a burden as I didn't want to be anywhere else. It was a work of love for me. I would have spent my life doing it if need be. And I could see the progress, so that encouraged me to go on.

My friends from the dancing world in America continued to be a rock of support and my guardian angels. Doireann Ní Mhaoiléidigh, and her twin Eimir, who flew in from Texas, would often drive four or five highways to get to me after her class, and many nights Doireann would stay with me in the apartment. Peter Smith and Patsy McLoughlin came over from New Jersey and spent weekends with me. My great friend, Laverne Showalter, flew over from Chicago to help me. Laverne, who had been a shoulder to cry on when I left Inis Ealga, was a great character and a tonic to have around in times of trouble.

Ian's friend, Paul Meyn, also came in from Kansas to spend a week with us. I remember two of my American-based friends, Terry Gillan and Philip Owens, were away in Europe, but they kept in constant contact by phone. On one occasion they said they were calling from a phone box on a street in Amsterdam, where they were visiting at the time. I was keeping a vigil at Ian's bedside at the time and little calls like that out of the blue kept me going.

And, of course, Barry came back to see his father, but it was very difficult for him as he had his own family to look after back in Scotland.

Ian continued having heart attack after heart attack in the hospital, but he was in the care of very good doctors. He'd had a defibrillator inserted and the alarms would go off when the numbers went up higher than they should; then there'd be an emergency situation. I remember one particular time they put me outside the room, but I could hear them trying to revive Ian with electric shocks. I couldn't bear it, so I walked way down the corridor, but I could still hear the shocks and Ian's shouts and screaming. I just didn't seem to be able to walk far enough away.

At this stage I was having lots of arguments with the Sacred Heart. Ian was having attacks more frequently, and they would go through that whole procedure with electric shocks. It was just awful what he was going through, despite all my prayers to the Sacred Heart. All those sounds stay in your head for a long time.

* * *

The weeks turned into months. I would go in early in the morning, take a break around 11 a.m. and go for a little walk, followed by a cup of coffee and a bun. Then I'd go back and stay with Ian until Doireann came in late at night.

Fortunately, Ian and myself had taken out very good insurance before our trip to America, so his medicals bills were covered. But coming up to three months, the insurance company was putting on pressure to have Ian moved back to the UK. However, the medical staff at St Joseph's were adamant that Ian couldn't be discharged until he had reached a certain level of fitness.

By now, Ian was also receiving physiotherapy in an effort to get him out of the chair and on to crutches. As soon as the physiotherapist was gone, I would continue working with Ian. This was my mission every day. I was going to have him walking.

I'd say to Ian, 'Okay, let's get up again and get going.'

Ian wasn't a lightweight, even though he was skin and bone at that stage. But a body isn't flexible, so it was quite an effort for me to get him up on sticks and teach him to put one foot in front of the other. We did that every day, as much and as often as we could.

Any programme that the occupational therapists or physiotherapists did became my programme for the day.

And it paid off.

The doctors were amazed by Ian's progress.

One day the neurosurgeon said to me, 'I never thought he would get to this point, but we are ready to let Ian go home.'

I was absolutely thrilled with that news. All along I had prayed to get Ian back home to England.

I knew it was going to take a miracle, but the Sacred Heart had finally come up trumps ... with lots of help from all of us.

THE FINAL JOURNEY

Now that Ian had been given the green light to return home to England, there was another major problem to surmount: finding an airline that would take him.

We searched around with little success. The main issue was having to remove three seats on a plane for the stretcher carrying Ian.

Some airlines were unwilling to make this adjustment to accommodate a stretcher, even though we had gold cover insurance.

I was very upset. We had been through so much heartache during the previous three months and I wasn't expecting this problem on top of everything else.

Thank you so much Canadian Airlines!

Finally, after an exhaustive search and much pleading with several airline companies, we were successful. Canadian Airlines had been really sympathetic to our plight and had no problem making the necessary alterations on the aircraft.

For the journey home, I was accompanied by my American guardian angel, Mary Cox, and a lovely nurse. This gave me great comfort as I had no illusions about the difficulties I was going to face on the trip.

Unfortunately, it wasn't a direct flight to London from LA. As we were travelling with Canadian Airlines, the first leg was to Toronto, where we had a stopover for ten hours. This would be an ordeal for people in the best of health, so you can imagine how torturous it was for poor Ian.

To make matters worse, the only place ground staff in Toronto could find to accommodate us with Ian on a stretcher was the airport chapel.

I flatly refused to spend ten hours in a chapel, despite being a religious person.

'Ian is not in a box, I'm not taking him to a chapel!' I told them in the middle of an argument.

Eventually, staff emptied out a store room and Ian was carried there on his stretcher. A wheelchair was also provided in case we needed it. Then the three of us did two-hour shifts watching Ian before going for little breaks to stretch our legs and clear our heads.

After what seemed like days, finally it was time to board the plane for the last leg of the journey home.

Ian's stretcher was manoeuvred into place on board, and the three of us took our seats across the aisle from him. Shortly after we took off Ian became restless, then agitated. Because of the height of the stretcher, he was very close to the overhead buttons for the airconditioning and service. When he became agitated he started pulling at the buttons and trying to take them apart. We had a constant battle to keep him from creating havoc.

It was like minding a troublesome little child.

At one stage the air hostess came down to me with a glass of champagne.

'You'll need a couple of these to get you through the flight,' she said.

And she wasn't wrong.

It was a horrific trip home, but poor Ian had no idea what he was doing. I had never been so relieved to hear the words 'prepare for landing' as we arrived at Heathrow Airport.

All three of us breathed a sigh of relief.

* * *

Michael Flatley and his company had organised a room for me at Berners Hotel on London's Oxford Street, and Ian was taken to the Devonshire Hospital off Harley Street to be assessed. It was only supposed to take a couple of days, but the consultant said that after the long journey Ian would need more time to recover.

I then spent my days at the hospital helping the nurses with Ian. By now I knew the routine, and it was second nature to me. And now the nurses were following my lead.

It was a very hot summer that year, and there was a lovely male nurse in the hospital who used to help me to take Ian out into the fresh air and sunshine in his wheelchair. We'd walk him up to Regent's Park and he was as happy as Larry. Ian loved Magnum ice cream bars, so every day we'd stop at an ice cream van and have a Magnum each. We'd spend a couple of hours out in the sunshine and it did Ian the world of good.

When his time was up at the Devonshire Hospital, Ian was then moved to an NHS hospital down by Canary Wharf, and then to London's Homerton

Hospital, where he received fantastic therapy. They specialised in brain damage, so we were very lucky to get Ian in there.

There were a lot of young people in Ian's ward who had been in motorbike and other road accidents, and it was awful to see the terrible injuries that had destroyed those young lives. The aim of the staff in that hospital was to get the patient into a fit condition to go home.

Ian would spend the next five months in Homerton.

At this stage the Irish dance teachers in London, Richard Griffin and Aaron Crosbie, were rallying around Ian and myself. Aaron introduced a mother in his school of dancing to me, a lady called Maggie Stapleton. Maggie is a very strong Catholic who believes in all the beliefs that we have. She was a good Christian at a time when I needed her in my life.

Maggie and her husband, Pierce, became good buddies with Ian. They would take him out of the hospital and wheel him around the streets of London to give me a break. And Maggie couldn't do enough for me. During that time we built a close and enduring friendship.

* * *

Michael Flatley then decided to form a second *Lord of the Dance* troupe to tour America. The company organised an apartment for me in London, so that I could work with Troupe 2, as it was called, while also being close to Ian.

My plan was to take Ian out of the hospital at weekends, so the apartment would have to be wheelchair-friendly. The company eventually located a suitable one in Kensington. It was a very nice, spacious, two-bed apartment, and it had a lift that could take the wheelchair up and down, so we would have easy access with Ian.

After months away from *Lord of the Dance*, I was now back working with a new troupe in London. Kelly Breen, the dancer from the Cathie Cosgriff school in Melbourne, Australia, who was with Ian and I when we went to see *Riverdance* in London, was now in Troupe 2. Kelly would regularly come and stay with me in the apartment for company. She was a wonderful young woman who was like a devoted daughter to me at that time.

Every day I would go in to see Ian and spend time with him. Then I'd leave for dance rehearsals with the troupe and set out work for them to do. I felt guilty when I was away from Ian, but in truth it was a break for me and I needed the interaction with other people. The dancers were a great comfort to me. They kept me sane: people like John Carey, Damien O'Kane, Jimmy Murrihy, Cian Nolan, Fiona Harold and, of course, Kelly Breen.

Kelly would leave rehearsals and go to the hospital to cover for me with Ian. I'm sure that wasn't necessary at all because the staff there were excellent, but I didn't want him to be on his own. Barry and Kim came down from Scotland and spent time with him as well.

When rehearsals finished at six in the evening, I'd take a bus back to the hospital. It was a very intense time for me. The dance troupe were amazed at how I could juggle my two lives: going to the hospital and burying myself in work with Ian, then going to dance rehearsals and burying myself in work with the dancers. And then returning to the hospital.

Ian's goal was to go home. Whether he knew where home really was I don't know. But he was always saying, 'I want to go home.'

His speech was very limited, but he would always get that sentence out.

Ian would also say, 'My wife!' in recognition when I'd walk into the room.

There were a couple of times when I walked in that he looked up and called me 'Iris'.

It never upset me because he would look at me with such love in his eyes.

On one occasion when he called me Iris, he actually said, 'I'm sorry.'

He knew he had made the mistake and that was good. It showed that his brain was finding its roots again, and the more I saw that the more I worked on it.

Eventually I felt that Ian was strong enough to spend weekends at the apartment. So I had my car brought down from Northumberland and I took on the crazy traffic in central London.

I'm sure I gave Kelly, Maggie and Pierce some scary moments as I weaved my way through the city, dodging cars shooting here and there.

My thoughts went back to my dear old Aunt Em and I cracked a smile as I remembered how she was terrified behind the wheel on empty Dublin streets in the early days. She'd never have survived the type of traffic I had to plough through in London.

Every Friday evening I'd drive to the hospital and we'd bundle Ian into the car with a wheelchair. I hired a nurse that I got to know at the hospital. She liked Ian and he liked her, so she would come out to the apartment every weekend and look after his medicines. If I had rehearsals at the weekend she would take care of him until I got back in the late afternoon. She'd dress Ian and take him out in the wheelchair.

Maggie and Pierce also came to stay at weekends with us. Ian and I shared the large bedroom, and Maggie and Pierce had the other one. Kelly would stay with the dancers. Maggie and Pierce found a little Catholic church in Kensington and they used to take Ian to Mass in the wheelchair on Sunday mornings to give me a lie-in.

One Sunday they returned from Mass with the shocking news that Princess Diana had been killed in a car crash in France. So I'll never forget where I was when I was told that Princess Diana had died. Like everyone else, I found that awful tragedy so hard to take in. It was a huge shock as I was a big fan of Diana. She was such a beautiful young woman, and her leaving her two boys behind was heartbreaking to think about.

It was a terribly sad time in London.

When Ian was back in hospital during the week, he was like a little child going to bed at night. For a while, if he wasn't asleep by the time I was leaving the hospital I would put up the side rails to stop him falling out of the bed. But as he improved, Ian would take down the rails.

Then I decided to get in beside him for an hour to relax him and get him off to sleep before I left at night. It worked, and soon the wives, partners and mothers of the other patients were doing the same, and we were all giggling.

Even though it was a very hard and sad time, there were lots of little laughs and smiles.

I wouldn't have got through it without my faith in the Sacred Heart. Despite the fact that I was having arguments over the cruel hand that had been dealt to me, I still turned to Him for help.

Ian was improving and constantly asking to go home, and eventually we found a wonderful rehabilitation centre called The Janie Heppell in Prudhoe that had five or six patients on one-to-one care.

We were blessed to get a place there.

And Ian went home.

* * *

We weren't long back in Prudhoe when Manuele Orto and his wife, Pam, from the Il Piccolo restaurant, took both Ian and myself under their wing. Somehow through the grapevine they had heard that something had happened to Ian while we were away in America. They were terribly upset, of course, because they were both very fond of Ian.

When we arrived back in London from the States, Pam got in contact by phone, and then she and Manuele came down to visit Ian in hospital. Even though they had busy lives running a restaurant and rearing their gorgeous son, Stefano, they still took the time to come and see us.

They were so kind and so supportive.

When Ian went to the rehabilitation centre in Prudhoe, Manuele and Pam became a constant presence in our lives, and I'll never forget their friendship and practical support during that period. They would regularly come down to the rehab centre in the afternoon before their restaurant opened and take Ian out for a walk around the beautiful grounds attached to it.

Other times they'd bring Ian for an afternoon drive, visiting places like the Angel of the North, the largest angel sculpture in the world, which is located a few miles from Newcastle.

Every evening Manuele would arrive in to the rehab centre with a special meal that he had cooked for Ian. Then he would personally feed him the lovely food, displaying the patience and love of a true carer.

Manuele and Pam were angels sent to me from Heaven. I will never be able to repay their kindness.

There were many times that Ian took a turn in the nursing home and had to be rushed to hospital. Each time I feared the worst, but he battled through like a resilient soldier.

Ian eventually got his wish to go 'home' that Christmas in 1997. His house was only three miles up the road from the nursing home. We pulled out all the stops to take him to his own home, and we fulfilled his wish.

I'm not sure if Ian realised that he was back in his own house, and we knew very quickly that he really wasn't up to being out of the nursing home, so we took him back two days later.

Ian was well enough the following 31 January for a trip to Il Piccolo where we gathered around him to celebrate his birthday.

'Romeo and Juliet' were back in their favourite restaurant – together.

Manuele and Pam organised a family table and everyone came. So Ian was surrounded by his family and people who loved him for his sixty-sixth birthday, even though he wasn't fully aware of what was going on.

Manuele and Pam wrapped their arms around me in so many ways. They could obviously see the toll that Ian's ill-health had taken on me. As a distraction, they arranged to take me to the theatre in Newcastle one Sunday night in March. They picked me up at the house and we popped into the nursing home on the way to Newcastle.

Ian was sleeping, and I gave the nurse on duty my mobile phone number, explaining where I was going. I think something or somebody was telling me that Ian's time was coming, because I remember having a strange feeling.

Sure enough, when I phoned the nursing home from the theatre at the interval, they told me they were just about to call me.

Ian had taken another turn and they were moving him to hospital.

Manuele and Pam drove me to the hospital straight away. The doctor who examined Ian informed me that he had pneumonia. They had given him antibiotics, so then it was a case of waiting to see if they had any effect.

Like the wonderful man that he is, Manuele stayed with me the whole night. He left the next morning to freshen up and change his clothes. Then sometime later he returned with fresh clothes that Pam had organised for me.

I sat by Ian's side all day that Monday, but he was unconscious and there was no sign of any improvement in his condition. That evening I looked down the corridor and I thought I was hallucinating. I could have sworn that I saw Maggie Stapleton walking in my direction. But Maggie was in London – or so I thought.

Sure enough, it was Maggie now standing by my side, with that lovely smile of hers.

'I just had a feeling and I had to come,' Maggie said, giving me a hug and kiss.

Manuele had contacted Barry, and he came down with Kim.

My brother, Brian, came over from Ireland with his son, Colm. They were all quite shocked to see how low Ian was at that stage. He drifted in and out of consciousness over the course of the week and into the following weekend.

Then the doctors came to me, Barry and Kim and told us that they were going to move him into a room of his own. It was at that moment we realised Ian's time was getting close.

We were now in a small but lovely family room. Ian wasn't conscious, and you could see the ominous signs: his hands were swelling and his colour was bad. But he was peaceful and surrounded by people who loved him, as we were all there with him over the next couple of days.

On the Wednesday night, as I was sitting by his side and resting my head on the bed, Ian suddenly opened his eyes, lifted his arm and patted my head. Then he closed his eyes again.

I believe in that strange but very special moment Ian was saying 'goodbye' to me.

It was the last time he was conscious.

At around five in the morning the nurses suggested that we adjourn to an adjoining room while they changed him and tidied up his bed.

Above: In 2003, Michael, Jimmy Murrihy and I found ourselves travelling VIP-style on Vladimir Putin's private plane from Saint Petersburg to Moscow, with a small group of passengers that also included Luciano Pavarotti and his wife!

Below left: Mike and my engagement party in 2003. Mike's cottage is in the background, and mine was next door. He built a beautiful archway, adorned with roses, in the fence separating the two! **Below right:** On the occasion of my sixtieth birthday in 2005.

Above, left and right: Myself and Mike at our wedding in the Haven Hotel in Sandbanks in January 2004, and me with Mike's daughters, Vicky Chapman (left) and Caroline Pask (right).

Below: Michael, Ronan and I take a bow at *Lord of the Dance* in the O2, Dublin.

Above: The cast of *Lord of the Dance: Dangerous Games* pictured at Castlehyde, Michael and Niamh's home at the time, in north Cork.

Below left: Myself and lovely granddaughters Chloe and Adele with Michael at *The Return of Michael Flatley* tour in Wembley.

Below right: Ronan and me at a Variety Club UK luncheon in London.

Above: In the music and dance centre of Limerick University rehearsing *Lord of the Dance: Dangerous Games*.

Right: Caroline Gray rehearses the lead role in *Dangerous Games* under the watchful eyes of myself and Michael.

Left: Rehearsals for the London Palladium performance of *Lord of the Dance: Dangerous Games*.

Right: Here I am leading a rehearsal for *Feet of Flames* in Taiwan. This show had 110 dancers in the cast.

Opening night of *Dangerous Games* at the Palladium in London.

Rehearsing 'The Lost Rose' from *Celtic Tiger*, in which the young couple dance a ballet *pas de deux* while Michael plays the flute.

Above left and right: My very talented student Ella Owens collecting prizes at the 2015 World Championships in Montreal and the 2016 Worlds in Glasgow. In the group photo are my fellow teachers Lucy English, Hilary Joyce Owens and Karen Nutley.

Above: The Céim Óir dancers at the 2016 Worlds.

Meeting Charles, Prince of Wales – twice! Left, Christopher Hannon from *Lord of the Dance* and I are introduced to him at the Prince's Trust dinner in Buckingham Palace, and below, I'm meeting Charles and Camilla at a private party at St James's Palace.

Below: The opening night of *Lord of the Dance: Dangerous Games* in the London Palladium.

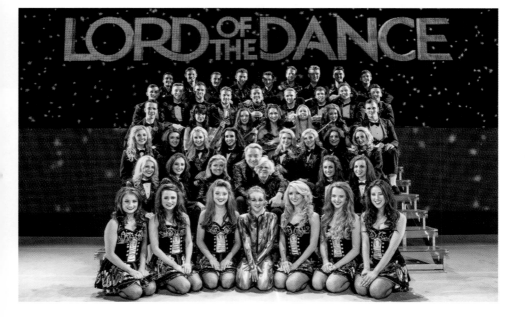

Above: Me giving a pep talk to Michael and the cast of *Lord of the Dance: Dangerous Games* before our show at the London Palladium.

Below: As we did many times over our twenty years working together, Michael and I share a quiet moment during rehearsals for *Celtic Tiger* in Birmingham.

They returned shortly afterwards and said, 'It's time to come in.'

We were all around him, friends and family, including his son Barry and daughter Lynda, as Ian passed away.

I felt that Ian's death was the most peaceful sensation in the world. I was holding his hand, saying some prayers and, maybe I was hallucinating, but I believe I sensed his soul leaving his body and going upwards. When I looked at him, Ian had a big smile on his face and he was very peaceful.

It was a very special and holy moment, and I felt very privileged to be there.

Afterwards, of course, I had to face the terrible, stark reality that my darling Ian was gone forever.

It was like the end of the world to me.

THE LAST GOODBYE

I an never realised the impact he'd made in the world of Irish dancing during the five short years he'd been in my life.

The teachers and dancers were all familiar with Ian Messenger, the dashing man who had swept Marie Duffy off her feet at the age of forty-five. Those who met him were charmed by his lovely, gentlemanly nature. They could also see the genuine love and passion he had for the dancing.

Not to mention how he adored me.

Flowers and messages came in from all over the world as the news spread that Ian had died. A lot of people were so shocked and upset for me. They knew that I had waited so long before I found happiness in my personal life, and then it had been so short-lived.

It would be two weeks before Ian's funeral took place, as is the norm in

England. I was in a daze for most of that time, but I had good people in my life to guide me and to help me take care of the arrangements.

When we were together and before he'd had the heart attack, Ian and I had often talked about dying. He always said that he wanted a big hooley and a big send-off. So I asked everybody to help me grant Ian that wish.

Another great passion of Ian's during his life was collecting malt Scotch whiskey. He had quite a collection of bottles and they were worth a lot of money. Ian had also said to me that he wanted them opened and enjoyed by family and friends at his funeral if he went before me.

Ian, as I mentioned earlier, loved coming to Mass with me in Crawcrook, the little town next to Prudhoe, on a Sunday morning, so I went to see the priest there to ask if it would be possible to have Ian's funeral Mass in that church called St Agnes's. The priest welcomed us with open arms.

The funeral service was everything that Ian would have loved and wished for: it was sacred, intimate and personal. We had our families and close friends there. Dance teachers came from Dublin, all over England and even America.

Our friend Manuele had insisted on hosting the reception after the funeral service, and afterwards we all went back to Il Piccolo to have a good old-fashioned hooley in Ian's memory.

Manuele had said, 'Just leave everything to me, I'll take care of it.'

I knew then that I didn't have to worry about how the day would go. Manuele laid on such a great spread in his restaurant, which he closed to the public that day. Ian's prized bottles of Scotch were opened and everybody drank a toast to him as the stories and memories flowed and laughter filled the room.

Afterwards people who were there would tell me that it was such a great funeral party.

So Ian had his final wish fulfilled.

* * *

I fell to pieces after Ian's death.

Even before he died, I wasn't in a good place. It's only now that I think back with horror to what I put people through at the time. I used to bore everyone to death talking about Ian, and the injustice and unfairness of what he was going through and how it had destroyed our lovely life together. I'd go on for hours and hours to anyone who would lend me an ear.

There was a therapist/psychologist in the rehabilitation centre in Prudhoe who recognised that I was in a bad way. 'I think you should come and visit me,' she said while Ian was there. I never did, but she could obviously see how much anger there was inside me.

My friend Mary Lyndsey knew a counsellor priest in Durham and she eventually persuaded me to see him after Ian died. At this stage I was crying day and night and I couldn't stop, so I agreed to seek this counsellor's help.

It was about an hour's drive from Prudhoe and Mary came with me the first time. After that visit, I decided to persevere with the counselling and I would travel on my own. But I'd spend the entire hour at the counselling session just crying.

One day, as I drove home to Prudhoe after seeing the counsellor, I heard police sirens. My instant thought was, 'Oh my God, there has been an accident!' Then I realised that the police car was behind me with flashing lights and trying to get me to pull in to the side of the road.

I stopped, and the policeman came up to the car. He looked at me and I was in floods of tears. He told me that my car had been swerving all over the place.

I had no idea that I had been driving erratically because I was lost in my world of grief. I was in such a bad state that I couldn't even remember the journey I'd just taken home from Durham. I couldn't stop crying, but I managed to explain to the police officer what had happened, how my husband had just died and how I was trying to deal with the heartache.

God love him, the policeman was really sympathetic and understanding. He was very kind and offered to lead me down to my house, which wasn't very far from where I had been stopped. But I then composed myself and assured him that I would be okay to drive the rest of the way on my own. And he allowed me to complete the journey.

* * *

I remember my brother Seamas asking *Lord of the Dance* manager Martin Flitton on the day of Ian's funeral to 'keep her busy'.

Seamas believed that thowing myself back in to work would help me through the dark days.

Within a month, Martin was on the phone to me saying: 'We have to get another troupe together for Las Vegas.'

Then he added: 'I know it's early days, but would it help if we found a studio up there in Newcastle?'

I told Martin I would be happy with that arrangement.

We did find a suitable studio in Newcastle, where over the following couple of months I drilled a new troupe of dancers who joined us for the next stage of *Lord of the Dance* – a residency at the New York-New York Hotel and Casino in Las Vegas. This would further consolidate the brand as the biggest dance spectacular on the planet.

It was a really exciting opportunity for all the young people who joined me in Newcastle as we prepared for that adventure. They were so pumped up and full of the joys of life, as young people should be going out into the world.

Immersing myself in the dancing, the choreography, the coaching and the show blotted out the pain while I was engaged with all of that. But, of course, there were quiet, solitary times when I was at home; that was when the tears would come, as I replayed the memories over and over in my mind.

Outside of my work I really was completely lost, but I had two angels in my life, Manuele and Pam, who made it bearable. They basically adopted me and were absolute gems.

I would be sitting at home alone in the evening and the phone would ring.

'What are you doing?'

The voice on the other end was Manuele.

'I'm on the computer,' I told him the first time.

'Stop it now and you come down or I go and get you,' he said in that lovely way he formed English sentences in his gorgeous Italian accent.

'Oh, don't worry, I'm fine, Manuele,' I lied.

'You be up in five minutes or I come down to collect you,' he insisted.

So I went up to the restaurant and he and Pam just engulfed me with affection and love and friendship. Their home was an open door to me, and still is to this day. Every evening at around 8.30 my phone would ring with the same invitation. And every evening I would join them in Il Piccolo.

I felt very comfortable in their company because Pam and Manuele were now like family to me. Manuele would make me laugh as he has a great sense of humour. I remember how one time, when Ian was alive, Manuele drove me to a feis. Some of my Irish dancing friends, Eugene, Brendan and Dan, who didn't know him at the time, saw us rolling up together at the venue in the car.

Manuele looked like a movie star behind the wheel, with his handsome features, leather jacket and dark glasses.

You could see them thinking, 'Who has Marie got on the side?'

During the feis one of the guys who was judging obviously couldn't contain his curiosity any longer.

He sidled up to Manuele and asked, 'So, who are you?'

'I am the bodyguard,' Manuele replied in a deadpan manner.

I burst out laughing.

Prudhoe and my friends anchored me during that awful time in the months after Ian died. I was glad to be there, and so grateful for the wonderful people who gave me support beyond the call of duty. They included Maggie and Pierce, who regularly came down to see me from their home in London.

People going through bereavement are always advised not to make any big life-changing moves for a while. I could have run away from Prudhoe, and even *Lord of the Dance*, but I realised later that that would have been a disaster for me. It was so important to stick close to my network of friends and to occupy myself with work that I enjoyed while I slowly worked my way through the grieving process.

Even though I had lost both my parents, the pain was nothing like I felt when Ian died. It was virtually unbearable grief, and I was told by the counsellor that while I could be living with it for a long time, this was quite normal. Grieving can take years because of all the stages you go through, from sorrow to loss, anger and even guilt.

I dealt with it over time thanks to a series of things, including the support of good friends, a job that I loved, and my religion. My faith and my devotion to the Sacred Heart played a big role. On visits home to Dublin I would go in to Whitefriar Street Church and spend hours in there praying, reflecting and doing my best to find a new sense of peace and happiness in my life.

Then suddenly I found myself caught up in a whirlwind as the offers for

Michael Flatley shows started arriving from all quarters.

Naturally, Michael was keen to capitalise on the demand for his dance shows.

As new deals were struck for *Lord of the Dance* performances of different shapes and sizes to be staged in a variety of venues, from Las Vegas to London's Hyde Park and Disney World in Florida, I didn't know what hit me due to the demands of training up the troupes.

This was the busiest time in my life, and the timing was perfect. I didn't have a minute to feel sorry for myself as life took over.

In a way, my prayers had been answered.

THE PRINCE AND THE

CLOG WITCH

The young dancers queuing up for auditions to join our new shows came from all over the world. But they had one thing in common: Michael Flatley.

To them, he was the face of *Riverdance* at the Eurovision Song Contest, and he was the star they aspired to be.

I heard from young hopefuls time and again at auditions that Michael Flatley was the guy they wanted to work with.

But in order to get to him, they had to get past me.

I was their first port of call. Every single dancer that we have had went through my hands. And I demanded total dedication, good discipline and a strong work ethic from them because of the standard of excellence that we required.

As a result of that, I did get a reputation for being strict and demanding. And I discovered at one point that the crew on *Lord of the Dance* had nicknamed me 'The Clog Witch'.

They would declare as I entered a building, 'Watch out, here comes The Clog Witch!'

But I would argue that any criticism I ever dished out was constructive and fair and for the benefit of the individual and the show.

There were times when I would be cross and tearing my hair out trying to get dancers to go the extra mile to achieve what we were looking for, and what I knew they could produce.

However, while I was tough on dancers, I was always conscious of delivering my message in a way that would never undermine their confidence. And I do think they respected that what I was doing wasn't being harsh with them for the sake of it; rather I was striving to instil a pride in their work and I was pushing them to bring out the best that I knew they had the ability to achieve.

In the decades that followed, I always received positive comments from the dancers I had worked with when they were moving on. I had letters and cards thanking me for the training and discipline that they got, and the experience and know-how they picked up in so many areas of work during their time with me.

So being 'The Clog Witch' maybe wasn't so bad.

They all laughed at that description of me anyway.

As I said earlier, I also became a substitute Mammy to the young dancers who joined our shows. *Lord of the Dance* was like a big family and I was their mother figure.

All through my life I'd had experience of working with children and teenagers in Irish dancing classes, but it was a lot more challenging and intense when I was out on tour around the world with young people. You hear parents talking about what they have to cope with during their childen's 'difficult teenage years'.

Well, welcome to my world.

We had all of that on the scale of a small army, but I'm happy to say both the teenagers and I survived it.

Here I have to point out that, fortunately, considering the amount of young dancers who worked with us, we never had anything serious to cope with. It was just the usual stuff you'd expect from teenagers struggling to find their feet in the world, never mind on the stage.

Parents entrusted us with their children, and I took that responsibility seriously. I remember one dance teacher handing me over her lively young teenage son in London with the words: 'Only it's you, Marie, I wouldn't let him go anywhere. I know you won't let him get out of hand. That's why I'm happy for you to take him in.'

It was a challenge for both of us, him as well as me, but actually that young fella turned out just fine. But everyone of the *Lord of the Dance* crew looked out for the young members of the cast. They were our assets and we never forgot our responsibility to them on a personal level.

The dance captains in *Lord of the Dance* were under strict instructions to contact me if any young dancer had a problem. If they were feeling sick or had any sort of small injury, they were not allowed to dance until they got a clearance that they were medically fit to perform. If a dancer had a minor trip or injury, he or she had to immediately pull out and be checked by the physiotherapist on duty. And if it was deemed that an X-ray was required, the dancer was immediately taken to a hospital or medical clinic.

That duty of care is something we took very seriously. I was on call twenty-four hours a day to deal with any problem like that.

As well as my role as mother, sometimes I was forced into the position of being an agony aunt, to the boys as well as the girls. We forget that boys are just as sensitive as girls.

However, I drew the line at mediating between couples who were having problems. I would listen, but I never took sides. I had quite a few broken hearts to deal with in my time, both male and female. But that's life.

There were many times when I was confronted with the problem of couples being split up to work in different touring troupes with *Lord of the Dance*. Whenever we brought in a new batch of dancers, we'd mix up the troupes so that each would have a good balance of experience to maintain the standard we set. Sometimes this would mean couples being parted, which didn't go down well. But we had made this clear when they joined up, so they understood that the show comes first.

Of course, there were times when dancers had the opposite problem after their relationships broke down. In that situation, they didn't want to be in the same troupe together, but they just had to deal with it.

Whatever personal issues were going on among the dancers, come show-time they were expected to set them aside and give the performance of their lives on stage. That's what people had paid good money to come and see. There are no sad days in show business. You have to banish them from your mind when the curtain goes up.

Michael Flatley was a typical example of that. When his father, Michael Snr, passed away in March 2015, in true show business tradition, despite his personal trauma and heartbreak, Michael went out and performed on stage in *Lord of the Dance: Dangerous Games* that same night.

* * *

Las Vegas is the entertainment capital of the world, so in July 1998, when we opened in our own theatre at the New York-New York Hotel and Casino, we knew that *Lord of the Dance* was now in the superstar league.

The *Lord of the Dance* venue wasn't a hotel showroom, it was an actual theatre that would become a second home to the young dancers over the following years.

It is hard to imagine what went through the minds of those young people when they first arrived in Vegas, which, of course, is also the gambling Mecca of the world. They were teenagers who had been plucked out of their normal, everyday lives, and transported to this bizarre planet that is Las Vegas.

I had held auditions for this new Vegas troupe in a venue at the top of Parnell Square in Dublin, and the response had surpassed all my expectations. The queue seemed to go on for miles, snaking down the street and around the corner that day. Those who made the cut were then taken to Newcastle where I trained them up. It was an intense experience for them – and now here they were in Vegas.

They seemed to quickly adapt to their new lifestyle. It helped that we were surrounded in Vegas by really decent people, from the hotel staff to the technicians and the theatre ushers to bus drivers. They all treated the young dancers like their own children.

I had mixed in some experienced dancers with the troupe and seconded Catriona Hale and Declan Bucke as dance captains for Vegas.

Our other dance captains, Bernadette Flynn and Daire Nolan, ran the European shows in Troupe 1. Bernadette Flynn, who came from Nenagh, Co. Tipperary, was just a schoolgirl aged sixteen when she first joined the show, even though she was a six-time world champion at that stage. She would go on to establish the character of 'the good girl' and make it her own as she developed it through the years.

Bernadette retired from the show in 2010, but even to this day girls taking her place aspire to the standard that she set for the role.

Before Vegas came around we had also put out a second troupe to tour around America, with a team of new dancers and some experienced members from Troupe 1, including John Carey, Jimmy Murrihy, Cian Nolan, Fiona Harold, Damien O'Kane, Areleen Ní Bhaoil and Gillian Norris. They were the leads and dance captains.

Back in Vegas the dancers got to enjoy the perks of being in a hit show on The Strip. It was VIP treatment for them all the way in the local clubs, where they could skip queues with their LOD badges. They were living a teenage dream, having the life of Reilly.

We did two shows nightly and we had to adapt the performance to suit our Vegas audiences, cutting it back to forty-five minutes and running through without an interval. Visitors to Vegas are mainly there to gamble, so if we had a break in the show there was every likelihood that they wouldn't come back. It's the nature of Vegas; there are too many distractions.

But the Vegas show was a tremendous success and it would run for four years.

The reputation of *Lord of the Dance* spread throughout the showbiz world and soon the show was attracting major celebrities. Singers Tom Jones and Shania Twain were among the first to check us out in Vegas, as was soccer legend Pelé. Tom Jones went out with the cast afterwards and he didn't stop raving about the show all night. Years later we went to see him in concert when we were in Paris, and he invited us to his after-show party. That night Tom was still talking about our Vegas show.

A lot of boxers came to see *Lord of the Dance*, probably because Michael had been a boxer and often talked about his love of the sport in media interviews. Mike Tyson was in the audience one night, and I hope we knocked him out with our performance. I just couldn't resist that!

Steve Collins, known as 'The Celtic Warrior' and one of the most successful fighters in Irish boxing history, was living in Vegas while we were playing at the New York-New York hotel. Steve came to see the show several times and would always come back and spend time with the cast when the show was over. One of our dancers, Jimmy Murrihy, reckons having us there made Steve feel that he was back in Dublin.

Wayne 'Pocket Rocket' McCullough, a champion boxer from Belfast, was living and working in Vegas when we later moved to the Venetian hotel, and the boys in the troupe played soccer with him a couple of times a week.

Speaking of soccer, the male dancers from Scotland started a Celtic Football Supporters Club in Las Vegas. Every week they would roam out into the small hours of the morning to watch Celtic matches on TV. I believe that their Las Vegas Celtic Supporters Club was even featured in the official Celtic magazine back home.

As the years went on our dancers grew accustomed to seeing famous faces in the audience at performances, and at the after-parties. It was always a thrill for all of us to meet celebrities. Michael Caine came to one of our early shows at Wembley Arena in London. Ian was still alive at the time and I remember him being very excited to meet that wonderful actor because he was such a huge fan.

Legendary American actor Jack Nicholson, singer Celine Dion and country superstar Garth Brooks also came to the shows in Las Vegas.

After we did a performance on their daytime TV show in the States, Donny and Marie Osmond were so excited and impressed that they later came to see the entire production.

Actress Goldie Hawn was at one of our London performances. Goldie came backstage and the female dancers had a great laugh with her. She was absolutely fascinated by their wigs and costumes, and she had a fit of giggles trying them on.

I'm not sure what my Aunt Em would make of this, but some of my own favourite memories are of meeting Prince Charles on several occasions when we performed for the Prince's Trust charity.

I always found Prince Charles to be a very nice man, who is quiet-spoken with a manner that is gentle and soft. And he came across as a person who had a genuine interest in other people.

After shows, Prince Charles would come down the line and have a word with each individual. And I noticed that he'd have a different comment or question for each person, so he showed genuine interest and it was very personal engagement. He wasn't going through the motions with stock comments.

I remember being nervous but very excited when I was introduced to him for the first time after *Lord of the Dance* had performed in James's Palace for a special event. The other entertainer that evening was the wonderful Shirley Bassey. Michael Flatley danced in the troupe that night and, of course, he made a massive impact on the room.

And then Prince Charles came down the line and we were introduced to him. He was very charming indeed that night.

Two years later, *Lord of the Dance* performed at a Prince's Trust event in Buckingham Palace and, once again, Prince Charles greeted us all individually in a line. When he reached me during the meet-and-greet his face displayed an instant recognition.

'Oh, I remember you,' Prince Charles said, smiling. 'You're the dance lady who works with him,' he acknowledged, referring to Michael.

That was good enough for me.

I was very chuffed indeed that I was now on Prince Charles' radar.

I was thrilled, in fact.

But Aunt Em was probably turning in her grave.

* * *

Michael's ambition kept on getting bigger in the wake of the success that *Lord of the Dance* was enjoying, particularly in Las Vegas.

As he said himself, he used to have a recurring dream about being on his deathbed and suddenly thinking about something he still hadn't done. Michael certainly didn't want that dream to happen, on either front.

So next he tells me that he has an idea for an open-air show called *Feet of Flames* to be performed in London's Hyde Park in July of that year, 1998.

'It's going to be a mega-sized show, everything has to be bigger and better and greater,' Michael said, his enthusiasm spilling out.

'We are going to perform it on three levels.'

My mind went into overdrive as I tried to imagine the scale of this new production. It was very exciting, particularly as Michael added that I would now have the challenge of working with 110 dancers who would be performing on the three levels at the same time. It would normally be thirty-six dancers in a regular show.

I didn't have time to draw a breath as we set about the creation of *Feet of Flames*. To pull off what Michael called 'the biggest show on earth', we combined Troupe 1 and Troupe 2. But we also auditioned another set of dancers, which we called Troupe X, and then we rehearsed them in Newcastle.

The newcomers who joined us for *Feet of Flames* included two of the O'Brien sisters, Niamh and Aoibheann. Troupe 3 stayed in Las Vegas.

There were huge changes to the set pieces from the original show, so the dancers had a lot to absorb and learn. And we drilled them to within an inch of their lives.

Feet of Flames was an incredible spectacle, with our army of dancers performing on three levels. We had fifty dancers on the floor in Planet Ireland. Above them were two shelves, as we called them, with thirty dancers on each shelf.

I knew that not everyone would be comfortable dancing on the higher levels, so the production manager, Barry Thornhill, the dance captains and I did our best to reassure the teams.

The dance captains and I had the cast watch while we went on the riser so that they could see how it moved up when we were on it. We did a couple of steps to show them that it was safe. We gave them a little demonstration on the different levels to help them banish any doubts or anxieties.

Unbeknownst to them I was feeling nervous about dancing on the higher levels myself, but I had to bite the bullet and do it. There were only a couple of dancers who had concerns and we had to change them around. I know of one dancer who went to a mentor and got some help for her fear of heights.

Hyde Park in July 1998 was an incredible day for everyone: the performers, the audience, Michael Flatley, and me.

I'll never forget it.

Several years down the road we would tour Taiwan with that show.

* * *

In those early years we were forever adding new dancers to cope with the demand for *Lord of the Dance* shows. But, as I said, we had no scarcity of talent coming through and bidding for a crack at the big time, or imagining themselves as the next Michael Flatley. Everywhere we went around Europe we held auditions and hired new people.

The next big residency we got was Disneyworld in Florida the following year. It was in July 1999, and was quite a challenge for the dancers, as they had to perform outdoors in sweltering heat. To help them acclimatise, we found a suitable outdoor spot where we did stretching and warm-up exercises, and then we got them to run through a full show under the blazing sun. It was a boot camp they had never before experienced. But show business is all about adapting to new situations and challenges.

As the grounds were open to the public during the day, we had to do the Disneyworld rehearsals on site in the middle of the night. So everyone was pulled out of bed at two in the morning, and then we'd work from three to six, going back home to our apartments after the sun came up. It was certainly a unique training regime. There was a lot of moaning and groaning at the start, but the dancers soon got used to it.

The Disneyworld performance was similar to our shows in Las Vegas, running for forty-five minutes with no interval. And they did two shows a day. After they settled in, the troupe loved working in Disneyworld and they enjoyed mixing and mingling with all the Disney characters.

One of our female dancers, however, had a nightmare experience when she was bitten by a spider one day in our costume department. The horrified dancer had to be immediately rushed to hospital, where, fortunately, it was discovered that the bite was neither life-threatening nor serious.

However, I'm sure the poor girl has nightmares about that incident to this day.

I still shudder at the thought of it.

* * *

Away from *Lord of the Dance* I had stayed close to my network of friends in Prudhoe after Ian died.

As I said previously, people going through a bereavement are advised not to make any life-changing decisions while they are recovering from their personal trauma.

Grieving sometimes takes years and you have to work through the various emotional stages of sorrow, loss, anger and guilt. This was the advice I was given.

Pam and Manuele's home remained an open door to me when I was back from my travels, and there was great comfort in that support. Having a dance studio in Newcastle so that I could commute to rehearsals while working on new shows also kept me anchored in Prudhoe.

My only brother living in England at this stage was Tony. He and his wife Lena were down in Dorset, in a town called West Moors just outside Bournemouth. My niece Cathy and her husband Len also lived down that way.

Whenever I was free I would drive down and spend weekends with Tony and Lena. As time moved on, they then suggested that I should consider relocating to their area so that we could be close to each other. And, after they planted the seed, I eventually came around to the idea and began house-hunting in that part of England.

Doing the rounds in my spare time viewing various properties for sale was an experience that I actually quite enjoyed. It was like a pastime. I eventually found a gorgeous house that captured my heart in a village called Three Legged Cross.

There were several explanations as to why this lovely little place is called Three Legged Cross. One theory is that a type of gibbet, known as a 'three-legged mare', was once common there; another suggests that once upon a time there was a boundary stone in the area, marking the convergence of three great estates: Lord Shaftesbury's to the west, Lord Normanton's to the north and east, and the nineteenth-century banking family Rolles-Fryer's to the south.

The main theory is that the name came from the road through the district, where it is divided into three separate stretches or 'legs'.

Whatever the reason, my dear friend Brendan O'Brien, who is a good joker, said that it was a fitting name for a choreographer's place of residence. But he would always refer to it as Three Crossed Legs!

Three Legged Cross was a very quiet area, but I did strike up an instant friendship with one of my immediate neighbours, Jane Born.

Jane had some horses and ran a horse riding school. We started off socialising over coffee and, of course, it was lovely to have somebody to talk to as I was still coming to terms with the loss of Ian, although the grief had greatly subsided.

One evening over a glass or two of wine we were discussing everything and anything when Jane suggested: 'We'll have to get you up on a horse.'

Now, at that point, I had never been near a horse in my life. But Jane insisted that it would be good for my head. I was more concerned about what it would do to my backside!

By the third glass of wine it began to seem more appealing and with gentle nudging from Jane I agreed to give it a go.

Of course, being a woman, my first thought was 'the look'. I would have to get kitted out in all the proper fashion. So that was a bit of fun, going off with Jane to buy all the gear.

Jane had a lovely old horse called Jonty, who was slow and gentle and reliable. Jonty and I got on very well from the start, even though my backside ached and my body creaked after the first few outings. But I soon got the hang of it and felt comfortable enough to be able to fully enjoy the experience as we sauntered up and down country lanes and quiet rural roads, chatting and admiring nature from our lofty positions on horseback.

Sadly, within the year Jonty took ill and I was devastated when Jane told me there was no option but to have him put down. That was the end of my short but very enjoyable horse riding experience, as Jane's other horses were too young and too frisky for me. I just couldn't take the risk of a fall.

At this point, I didn't have any contact with my other neighbour, a gentleman who lived in a lovely cottage next door. I caught a glimpse of him a couple of times on the rare occasions that he was at home while I was back in the area, but we never bumped into each other in person.

Little did I suspect what would transpire between the neighbour in question, Mike Pask, and me.

THE NEXT-DOOR

NEIGHBOUR

I moved to my Three Legged Cross home in March 1999. It was at the start of a very busy year working with Michael Flatley, so I didn't get around to organising a house-warming for family and friends until the following December.

One of the people I decided to invite to the party was the man next door, even though I still hadn't met Mike Pask in person at this point.

The evening before the event I slipped into a warm coat and walked briskly to his cottage during a break in the deluge of rain that had come tumbling out of the heavens over the previous few days.

It seemed like an eternity before the door was opened by a very tall man who appeared to be distressed and didn't seem at all pleased to see me standing on his doorstep.

I took a deep breath, forced a smile and introduced myself. My neighbour seemed really distracted as I spilled out my invitation to the house-warming.

He muttered something about the weather, and then he declined my invitation, saying he would be away visiting his daughters the following evening.

So, I said 'that's fine' and off I went with my tail between my legs, thinking that my next-door neighbour, Mr Pask, was a very grumpy man indeed.

What I didn't know then, but would learn later, is that Mike had just returned home from a business trip in France to find that there had been a major leak and there was a flood in his cottage.

It's all about timing in life, and my timing certainly wasn't very good that evening.

* * *

The next couple of years passed in a whirl due to my work with *Lord of the Dance*. It was a full-on job keeping the shows running smoothly around Europe and in other parts of the world. There was always some little incident throwing a spanner in the works.

I remember one time turning up for a show in Germany only to discover that a box containing all the shoes for the dancers had been stolen. Alarm bells started ringing all over the place as we battled against the clock to avert a disaster. There would be no show that night without shoes. In the end, our manager Martin Flitton saved the day. I don't know where he found the magic wand, but Martin produced dancing shoes before the curtain went up that night.

There was another bizarre incident during a show in Germany when a naked guy ran across the stage behind a line of dancers. It transpired that the streaker had been one of the local riggers working on the show. He was fired on the spot. But it gave us a laugh.

On my short trips home to Three Legged Cross, I noticed that Mike was rarely at his cottage. Then there was a period when I'd see him building something in his garden whenever he was around. It turned out that he was constructing a yacht. Mike's passion was sailing, I later discovered, and he'd be out on the sea every chance he got when he wasn't working.

In May 2003 I was having some repair work done on my garden pond, which was my pride and joy. It had lots of fish, including three or four really big ones. There was a problem with water escaping, and a couple of guys from the local garden centre had been sorting it out for me to save the fish. Even though it was the start of summer, it was a windy morning and, to my horror, as they drove away my front door slammed shut behind me with the keys inside. Because it was early morning I hadn't opened up any of the side or back doors, so now I was locked out of my house.

My niece Cathy and her husband, Len, who lived just five miles away in the village of West Moors, had a spare set of keys to my home. However, I couldn't phone them because my mobile was inside, as were the keys to my car.

After my initial panic subsided, I decided to go next door and ask Mike if I could use his phone to call Cathy. I had to summon up all my courage because I hadn't met him since that December night a couple of years previously, when I got what I considered to be a frosty reception on his doorstep. There was no answer when I knocked on his door, and then I noticed that there was no car at the house so I turned to leave. As I was walking away, he drove in from a back entrance.

This time Mike Pask was a lot friendlier than the man I had first met. I explained my predicament and asked if I could use his telephone to call my niece.

'Of course, no problem, come on in,' he said. 'Have you tried all the doors of the house?' I told him there had been no point as I hadn't unlocked any of them that morning.

When I phoned Cathy she told me that Len had possession of the keys, but he was now in America on business.

'I don't know where he's put them, but I'll have a good search,' she said.

In the meantime, Mike kindly offered to drive me to West Moors to pick them up. When we got to Cathy's home there was more bad news. Cathy had searched high up and low down for the keys without success. Finally, she had phoned Len in America. I'm sure that poor Len must have thought there was an awful disaster back home when he received a call at that time.

Len told Cathy that the keys to my house were in his car, which was parked at Heathrow Airport!

I was really embarrassed going back out to Mike and informing him that our trip had been in vain. He could see that I was now in a bit of a state. I told him that I was due to fly out to Russia the following morning with *Lord of the Dance*.

'Oh don't worry,' Mike assured me. 'We'll see if there's a window we can break and we'll get it sorted.'

Back at the house, Mike started trying the various doors at the side and rear.

'I don't think there's any point in doing that as I didn't have a chance to open them this morning,' I told him again.

But he went around checking the doors and finding each one locked as I expected. Then there was one last door next to the garage and, lo and behold, to my embarrassment it opened when he turned the handle.

I was mortified and instantly apologised to Mike for all the inconvenience I'd put him through. But he just laughed and insisted that it had been no trouble.

Of course, to this day Mike tells people that the whole saga that morning was just a ploy to reel him in.

* * *

My trip to Russia the following day was no ordinary one. I was off to the 300th anniversary celebration of the founding of St Petersburg, where *Lord of the Dance* had been invited by President Vladimir Putin to perform at the opening ceremony. Michael had chosen the 'Warlords' number from the show, featuring the boys.

That was a very memorable trip for me. Our troupe performed in front of the most powerful people in the world at that time: including Putin, President George W. Bush, British Prime Minister Tony Blair, President Chirac of France, Germany's Chancellor Schroeder, and Irish Taoiseach Bertie Ahern.

We felt immensely proud that our taoiseach was there.

As well as *Lord of the Dance*, the entertainers included Nana Mouskouri, Demis Russos and the great Pavarotti.

After the event, Michael Flatley, dancers Damien O'Kane and Jimmy Murrihy, and I had a pre-planned trip to Moscow to do a workshop for a Russian Irish dance school called Iridian. It was the only Irish dancing school in Russia at that time and had been founded by a guy called Igor Denisov, who told us that he set it up after being inspired by a video of *Lord of the Dance*. He had even learned Michael's steps. Igor had a hundred dance students at that time.

What happened next is like something from a movie: President Putin then offered us a lift to Moscow on his private jet. And so Michael, Damien, Jimmy and I found ourselves travelling VIP-style on the Russian president's private plane with a small group of passengers that also included Luciano Pavarotti and his wife!

* * *

Mike was on my mind when I was returning from Russia. I felt the urge to buy him a gift as a token of my gratitude for his help the day before I had left, so I decided on a bottle of Russian vodka.

When I settled in back home I organised a little get-together over a barbeque with Cathy and Len, their children, and my friends Maggie and Pierce.

That same afternoon I noticed that Mike was in his garden working on his boat, so I called him over and gave him the little gift of vodka.

'We're having a barbeque at the moment – would you like to come and join us?' I added.

'Oh, thank you very much, but I've just eaten,' Mike responded in a tone that wasn't dismissive. I then suggested that he drop in for a drink whenever suited him, and he was happy to accept.

Mike came around later and he was very sociable and engaging. We all enjoyed his company and the evening went by all too quickly, as good times do.

Today, Mike says he crawled home that night after we'd had several bottles of wine, followed by Irish coffees which I had insisted on making for him.

'My friends say I make a mean Irish coffee,' I told him that night.

'Okay, well I'll have to try one then,' he laughed.

Three Irish coffees later, Mike went home in a very happy mood. And so our relationship went on from there.

Mike later told me that he felt an attraction to me during that evening at the barbeque, assuring me that it had nothing to do with the bottles of wine that were consumed.

I was out in my garden a couple of weeks later when he called me over.

'Would you like to go out for a meal some evening?' Mike asked.

I didn't have to think twice about it.

'Would tomorrow evening suit you?' Mike then enquired.

So the following evening Mr Pask arrived through my gate, all scrubbed up and looking very smart indeed for our date. Mind you, it wasn't easy to spot him through the jungle of colourful flowers cradled in his arms.

Shortly afterwards a taxi arrived and I was whisked off to a very nice restaurant out in the countryside that I'd never been to before. It was a lovely 'getting to know you' evening as we discussed our lives up to that point over good food and wine.

Mike told me that he was an only child and had been born on the Isle of Wight. His father was an army man and they moved around when he was a child, at first living in Surrey and then in Kent, where he spent his schooldays. That experience of pulling up roots and moving on would shape the course of his own life. Mike said he never stayed in the same house for more than seven or eight years, even during his first marriage. He'd buy houses, do them up, and then move on.

Mike, at this point, was divorced with two grown-up daughters, Caroline and Vicky. He had been married for over twenty-five years before his separation and divorce. Mike told me that he and his wife had drifted apart during their lives, as some couples do, and the split came after their children were reared.

Their parting was obviously an emotionally draining experience, like any divorce. But Mike said it was an amicable separation, one that he and his then wife dealt with between them, rather than going down a legal route. Thankfully, they are still on good terms, and today they meet up whenever there is a family event that brings them together. Mike's wife has since remarried.

Mike was well travelled. He was a chemical engineer who worked abroad as well as in the UK. In the 1970s, he spent several months on an assignment in Brazil. He had bought his cottage at Three Legged Cross, about three or four miles from his family home, after the split with his wife. The reason I didn't see a lot of him when I moved in next door is that he was working on a £20 million project for a big American company called Borden Chemicals.

At that time Mike was overseeing the shutdown of their plant in Southampton and the installation of their new manufacturing facility in Barry Island in Wales. He also had responsibility for their operating plants in France, Holland and Spain. He was a busy man during those years.

The pressure valve for Mike during his hectic working years was his love of the sea and sailing. The project I'd observed him building in the years after I moved in next door was his pride and joy: a 33ft yacht called *Out of the Blue*.

That evening together just flew by and I recall thinking how Mike was such good company, very pleasant and with a great sense of humour. There was good chemistry between us, he made me laugh, and upon our return home we both agreed that we'd go out again.

I was due to head off on another *Lord of the Dance* trip, so we promised to make arrangements when I returned.

After I got back, Mike invited me for a day out on his beloved yacht, which was now in swinging moorings in Sandbanks at the mouth of Poole Harbour. That outing was arranged for a couple of days later, depending on the winds.

I was very excited as this felt like a very glamorous adventure indeed, even though I knew nothing about boats.

As luck would have it, weather conditions were perfect when the day arrived for our jaunt on the sea. Mike collected me in his car and chauffeured me to where the yacht was moored.

It was all going very well at this point and I was really enthused about the sea trip that lay ahead, but then I noticed the look of horror on Mike's face as I was about to step on to his boat.

That was the moment he realised I was still in my stilettos. To a sailor, I would learn, strutting around in stiletto heels on a yacht is a major crime. I know now, of course, that it certainly wasn't very practical.

Mike must have thought I was very stupid, but fortunately I redeemed myself immediately by producing freshly made sandwiches and a couple of bottles of wine that I had taken with me for the trip.

At that point I didn't know Mike's taste in vino, but I had chosen Chablis and Châteauneuf-du-Pape.

And I had obviously chosen well, because judging by the smile on Mike's face my faux pas with the stilettos was quickly forgiven, although it would never be forgotten.

I still get teased about it to this day.

That lovely day together out on Mike's yacht, *Out of the Blue*, put the wind in his sails, as they say, and then there was no stopping him.

Two months after we got together, and literally out of the blue, Mike Pask popped the question!

A WHIRLWIND ROMANCE

In mid August 2003, Mike took me out for a lovely afternoon exploring around the Isle of Purbeck in Dorset, which is a picturesque peninsula and a very romantic area.

One of the attractions is Old Harry Rocks, three famous chalk formations. There are various accounts about the naming of the rocks.

One legend says they were called after Harry Paye, the infamous Poole pirate whose ships hid behind the rocks waiting to pounce on unsuspecting passing merchants.

Another tale has it that a ninth-century Viking raid was foiled by a storm and that one of the drowned, Earl Harold, was turned into a pillar of chalk.

Some say that the devil, known euphemistically as 'Old Harry', had slept on the rocks.

It was a beautiful sunny Sunday when we took the chain ferry at Sandbanks, with neither a pirate ship nor a devil in sight. The walk up to Old Harry is really idyllic with breathtaking views, and that day the blue sea was shimmering under a glorious sunny sky.

I felt really comfortable with this new man in my life. Somebody was looking out for me because I was so happy again. But I wasn't prepared for the proposal from Mike when he sprung it on me that evening.

I was speechless for a few moments. Even though we'd been seeing each other every day for two months, marriage hadn't crossed my mind at that stage. I was just enjoying having a lovely relationship again.

Mike was adamant that he wanted to marry me, explaining that he had no doubts about his commitment to me. And because he was aware of my strong Catholic beliefs, he said he felt that it would be unfair to ask me to move in with him outside of marriage.

Bless him.

I thought about it for a minute.

And then I said, 'Yes! Yes! Yes!'

As we talked it over we both agreed there was no point in hanging around. We weren't teenagers, so why wait for a couple of years?

Before Mike popped the question, we had already booked a long weekend in Rome, so we decided to do the formal engagement during those few days in that most romantic of cities. Before that, there was a trip to Hatton Garden in London for one of those exciting events in a woman's life: choosing a ring. It all happened so fast that I felt I was in some kind of a fairy tale.

The icing on the cake was the reaction from Mike's two daughters, Caroline and Vicky, who I had met at this point. They were delighted for us when their dad broke the news.

* * *

Like everything in my hectic life, the next challenge was to arrange a wedding around my commitments to *Lord of the Dance*.

There was a lot going on that summer with the show playing during July and August at the Bournemouth International Centre, which was very convenient to where we were living.

That August in 2003 *Lord of the Dance* had also been invited to perform at Prince Albert's Red Cross Ball in Monte Carlo in front of an audience that also included Prince Rainier and Princess Caroline.

I brought Mike with me, the new man in my life who I couldn't wait to introduce to my other 'family' as I call the people I've worked with in *Lord of the Dance*.

Michael Flatley was on stage rehearsing that day for the performance when I arrived in with Mike. The word was already out that we were getting married.

When Michael spotted the two of us in the distance I could see his face light up. Then he leapt off the stage, raced at us and gave Mike the biggest hug and the warmest welcome.

That moment hadn't been rehearsed, but it couldn't have gone any better.

Mike remembers that day as a daunting experience for him, and says he felt intimidated by it. He could design chemical plants and run a £20 million project, but *Lord of the Dance* and the world of show business was completely alien to him. Now here he was mixing with royalty and celebrities in Monaco, and you forget what it is like being involved in something like that the first time. By then, even though I didn't take it for granted, it was a normal working day for me. It was only afterwards when we spoke about it that I understood what it meant to Mike.

The show was spectacular. Shirley Bassey was on the bill that night, performing one of her signature big numbers, 'Diamonds Are Forever'. And former James Bond star Roger Moore, still looking a million dollars in his twilight years, was among the glitterati.

That summer, at the end of our *Lord of the Dance* season in Bournemouth, we hosted an engagement party in the garden of my home in Three Legged Cross and a huge number of the dancers came along to help us celebrate our personal event.

Mike couldn't stop smiling.

Later, when friends would ask him what he did on tour with *Lord of the Dance*, he'd tell them that he carried the bags.

Then he'd add: 'But I've got the best job in the world because I'm surrounded by all these beautiful women.'

* * *

Our wedding day was finally booked for 3 January 2004, when there was downtime in *Lord of the Dance*.

In the meantime, I was flying all over the place working on the show and keeping up with all my other activities in Irish dancing.

Mike and I were still living in our respective homes at this stage. One day I returned from a short trip away with *Lord of the Dance* to find that he had constructed an archway, adorned with roses, in the fence separating our houses. And there was a statue of Venus, the goddess of love, on the other side.

Although he'd never admit to it, Mike is a true romantic.

If you asked him about the romantic archway today, he'd tell you that it was for practical reasons. It allowed access to both houses without us having to walk by the side of a busy road. Of course, that was the end result, but there was romance at the heart of it.

As well as sailing, another passion of Mike's is gardening. I remember arriving home from abroad on another occasion to find a splash of rose beds planted in my garden as a surprise for me. There was another personal touch: the roses were white and yellow, the colours of the Vatican flag. Mike had chosen them knowing my devotion to the Catholic religion.

It was so lovely to come back to all of those different surprises from Mike during that period in the summer of our romance.

Our wedding the following January played out over an entire weekend, as every good Irish wedding should. Mike and I were joined by our families and friends from all walks of life during those unforgettable few days. I was delighted that my late husband Ian's son, Barry, was able to join the celebrations with his wife, Kim, and their son, Ian Jnr. Angela Meleady and family, who had been such a big part of my life, were there too.

We had Mike's daughters, Caroline and Vicky, and their families. Caroline and her partner Lee were accompanied by their children, Adele and Kieran. Vicky and her husband, Mark, attended with their children, Aaron and Chloe. It was a real joy for Mike to be surrounded by his children and grandchildren at that special time.

It was also so lovely for Mike that his ninety-six-year-old dad was able to attend the wedding despite being in poor health. He was a real gentleman who made me feel very welcome when Mike first introduced me. Sadly, he passed away two years later.

As well as his family, Mike was also surrounded by quite a bunch of his friends, going right back to his schooldays, as well as those he had met through his own career.

Of course, we had our mutual friends that included my extended family in *Lord of the Dance*, my Irish dance friends and teachers from all over Ireland and England, plus Irish dancing adjudicators from every country.

We kept the airports busy with people flying in from all over the world. The Ryanair plane from Dublin to Bournemouth was fully booked by our Irish guests. And there was a constant flow of shuttle buses to Heathrow Airport picking up those who made the journey across the Atlantic from North America.

My good friend Laverne Showalter travelled all the way from Chicago with her daughter, Julie.

When she arrived into the hotel, Laverne announced in a grand manner: 'The mother of the bride is here!'

Laverne was such a wonderful character. She has since passed on and I really miss her in my life today.

Naturally, when I was planning our big day my choice was to marry in a Catholic ceremony. I went to see the priest in my local church, but he told me they couldn't do it because Mike was divorced. Of course, I knew this would be the answer, but it was worth a try. Instead, our beautiful ceremony took place in a Chuch of England church in nearby Verwood.

My nephew, Len, gave me away, as the saying goes. Being a Glaswegian, Len decided to mark his heritage by wearing a traditional kilt, and he brought along his nephew from Scotland to serenade me on the bagpipes as I entered the church, and again later as I emerged from that house of worship with my new husband.

Orfhlaith Ní Bhriain was our singer at the ceremony and she added so much to the experience. Orfhlaith has the most gorgeous voice and her rendering of Ave Maria is very haunting and moving to hear. This was Orfhlaith's second time to sing at a wedding where I was the bride, as, of course, she had also travelled to Kansas for my marriage to Ian.

When we emerged from the church as man and wife, Michael Flatley was among the first guests to congratulate us and shower us with big hugs and kisses in that warm way he greets people.

The Haven Hotel at the tip of the Sandbanks Peninsula in Poole was the venue for the wedding reception that followed. It was Mike's hotel of choice for our wedding day. In the years when he was out on his yacht, Mike would pass The Haven which sits on the water at the entrance to Poole Harbour. It always had a place in his heart.

It is a hotel with a lot of history as it was home to the Italian inventor and physicist, Guglielmo Marconi, from 1898 to 1926. Marconi, of course, invented radio and established wireless communication between France and England across the English Channel. There is a Marconi Lounge in The Haven with lots of old photographs from his time living and working there with his family.

Marconi had a reputation for hosting big communal family meals when he was residing there, and we certainly carried on that tradition on our wedding day. There was great food, lots of champagne and endless bottles of wine, plus singing and dancing into the early hours of the following day.

After the champagne corks popped at the reception before our meal that day, Michael Flatley had a surprise wedding present for Mike and I. He escorted us outside to the hotel forecourt where a two-seater Mercedes SL convertible was wrapped in an enormous pink bow.

During the evening I made a little wedding speech stressing how blessed Mike and I felt to be surrounded by our families and great friends from all the different areas of our lives that day.

As the hours slipped from night into morning the party never sagged. Marconi may have invented radio, but nobody creates a hooley like the Irish and our friends when we all get together.

The Maldives in the Indian Ocean was the paradise where we then spent our honeymoon. The island we stayed on was just like heaven on earth. We spent our days walking barefoot in the sand and soaking up the sunshine, while our nights were all about romantic dinners. The sea temperature was like a warm bath. I wanted to stay there forever.

It was the perfect start to our new life together as man and wife.

* * *

Although both my marriages came late in life, I had a lot to be thankful for. I made a very good choice when I married my first husband, Ian. The five years that followed were blissful. I was never happier. And I never thought I'd get a second chance to have that kind of life after he died.

They say that lightning never strikes twice. Well, I'm happy to say that it does.

Mike is the most wonderful husband and we've had a lovely life together since we wed. Of course we have our little arguments like normal people do, but they're always minor issues. Mike can be very stubborn and I don't always get my own way, but we know how to compromise. We are different people, but at the same time we complement each other.

He is a very sociable person and he's good at entertaining people. When we first got together he had no interest in cooking, but now he's king of the barbeque.

Mike never had a problem fitting into the Irish dancing world and was immediately welcomed with open arms. Although it was all new to him, he then accompanied me to the feiseanna and the international championships.

Sometimes, of course, he'd find it a bit tedious sitting in a hall watching competitions, and he'd slip away.

But I understand that.

Mike loves cricket and I'm not the biggest fan, so I find other things to do when he's watching it on the television. It balances out.

Today, I can't imagine my life without Mike.

He has been by my side during all of the highs and lows that we've experienced since walking down the aisle.

As the wedding vows say, Mike married me 'for better or for worse'.

It is easy to sail along happily in the good times. But the real test of a person and of a relationship comes in the days when the going gets tough.

And that challenge started the day I went for the results of a cancer test.

TIME FOR CHAMPAGNE

'I have to tell you that we have found breast cancer.'

They're the words every woman prays she'll never hear in her lifetime.

Sadly for me in July, 2010, that was my diagnosis. It was a huge shock, but what sent me into a total spin that awful day was the further revelation that my cancer was at an advanced stage.

Of course, dark thoughts that I was going to die crossed my mind in that moment. But I brushed aside that possibility, stopped thinking about it, and immediately decided to face this challenge with a positive attitude. There is no other way to deal with it. The alternative is to give up without a fight. And I certainly had no intention of doing that.

'This is a bummer, but that's life,' I thought.

* * *

Going back, I always had my breast check carried out every two years in England. The NHS covers all women over the age of forty for breast cancer screening, which is just great. But I had missed my last appointment due to moving house and relocating to the Poole area and it had slipped my mind after that.

Then, in December, 2009, eight months before my diagnosis, I was over in Dublin attending a Coimisiún meeting, and when I came out of the shower one morning I noticed what looked like a scar or a line across my right breast. I wasn't alarmed because it didn't look like anything serious, there was no pain or discomfort, and I thought maybe it had been due to my sleeping position in the bed that night.

It didn't go away, but I still wasn't too concerned about it. I'm not the sort of person who goes running to the doctor with every little ailment, so I let it pass for a few months.

However, when it was still there in July, I decided to go to my GP, just to be on the safe side. I still didn't have any worries because I was feeling on top form. I was fit and healthy and working really hard with *Lord of the Dance* at the time.

My GP, a lovely doctor, examined me and I got no sense of anything sinister coming down the line.

'How long have you been harbouring this?' he asked in a tone that didn't alarm me in any way.

When I explained that I had first noticed the mark the previous December, he nodded and continued the examination.

'It may be nothing,' he said. 'But to be on the safe side I'm going to fast-track you to have it thoroughly checked out.'

Within ten days I was in the Ladybird Clinic in Poole Hospital where I had a biopsy and a series of scans and tests. I was under a consultant called Abigail Evans, whom I didn't see that day, but the attention I received from her team was second to none.

Afterwards, they told me that it would take up to two weeks before they would have the results. However, about a week later I received a notice that my results were back and there was an appointment for me to come in and see them.

Mike came with me, and the moment we walked into the room we both instantly knew that the news was bad. The entire team was gathered there, all of them with solemn expressions on their faces. I was then informed that I had a high grade of breast cancer.

Mike piped up and asked, 'Does this mean surgery?'

'Yes, it will require a mastectomy,' came the reply.

We both took deep breaths as this news sunk in.

Before going in that day, Mike and I had discussed what we would do if there was a serious problem. We have private medical insurance, so we agreed that we would go down that route because it's speedier.

The leader of the medical team said I needed to be treated immediately, but that they couldn't take me for six to eight weeks.

With our private insurance we were able to stay with the same consultant, Abigail Evans, who had a vacancy on her private list and was able to give me a booking within ten days.

In fact, we were able to see her that very morning.

Abigail is a straight-talking woman. She doesn't beat about the bush when it comes to outlining your situation. Some would say that she hasn't got a very good bedside manner, but Abigail's response is that she's there to save your life.

So Abigail didn't hold back, telling me how bad my aggressive cancer was, and then filling me in on what lay ahead: there would be more tests, a biopsy, at least six treatments of chemotherapy, followed by radiotherapy, and then eleven months of Herceptin treatment and reconstruction further down the road.

As the information poured out, it was quite a shock to Mike and myself and lots of deep breaths needed to be taken.

Then Abigail added: 'I can take you in next week, I have a vacancy.'

Despite the shock of the diagnosis and the awful picture of what lay ahead for me, I had another concern. I was booked to go to Dubai with *Lord of the Dance* that week.

'Well, one more week won't make any difference,' Abigail replied when I told her about my commitments.

'You go and do what you need to do and I'll take you in a few days after you get back.'

That was a day neither Mike nor I will ever forget.

We didn't know if the cancer had been caught in time, or if it could be cured. This was something that was in the lap of the gods. But we both decided there and then that we would do our best not to let the cancer control us. It was going to have to fit in with our lives.

On the way home that day we stopped off at The Harbour Heights Hotel overlooking all of Poole Bay.

'Time for champagne!' I said.

And so began a lovely ritual that would continue all through my cancer operation, treatment and recovery. Through the bad days and the good ones, Mike and I would stop off at The Harbour Heights and have our bottle of champagne on our way home.

Cancer wasn't going to deprive us of that little pleasure.

* * *

The trip to Dubai for the staging of *Lord of the Dance* at a big corporate event helped to take my mind off my personal worries as I focused on the show, although I must admit that I was going through an emotional roller coaster as I knew what I was facing when I came back.

In Dubai, I confided in some of the key members of the troupe, and naturally they were quite shocked.

Michael Flatley wasn't with the troupe and after the show I phoned to tell him how it went.

'I have some good news and some bad news, Michael,' I said.

There was a pause at the other end of the phone.

'I'll give you the good news first,' I added.

So I told Michael that the performance had gone without a hitch and the dancers had enjoyed standing ovations.

'So what's the bad news?' Michael then asked.

'I have a little problem,' I said hesitantly, feeling myself well up with emotion.

Then I told him: 'I have been diagnosed with breast cancer and I have to go into hospital next week for a mastectomy.'

I could hear him gasp on the phone. Michael immediately offered to help in any way he could.

I assured him that I was fine and that everything would be okay.

'I'll be out of action for a couple of days after the op, but I'll be back at the auditions next week,' I said.

Michael was surprised by this and urged me to take as much time as I needed to recover and to get back to full health.

At this stage we were starting the preparations for a major tour that was generating huge excitement among fans because it was going to feature Michael dancing in the production again after a break of thirteen years.

'Michael Flatley Returns as *Lord of the Dance*', the adverts declared. The timing of my cancer couldn't have been worse from a professional point of view.

Speaking with Michael that day I could hear his genuine concern for me. He said he would be praying for everything to go well with the operation and would keep in regular contact with Mike, which he did. Michael and his wife, Niamh, kept in constant communication throughout the whole procedure.

My husband Mike had accompanied me on the trip to Dubai and he kept my spirits up during that trip. It was only on the last night that he let his guard down. We were in an outside bar at our gorgeous hotel, and the people in the show who were aware of my diagnosis and impending surgery were coming up to me and wishing me luck. After everyone had gone and it was just the two of us having a glass of wine, Mike broke down and sobbed.

People tend to forget what a partner or spouse is coping with in those situations. In our case it was fear of the unknown, as the prognosis wasn't good. The medical team didn't paint a bright picture to either of us, so the Sacred Heart had a lot of work to do.

My operation was carried out on a Wednesday in BMI The Harbour Hospital, a private hospital run by BMI Healthcare, and I was brought in the night before and prepped. I was taken to the theatre early the following morning and given an anaesthetic. When I woke up four or five hours later it was all over. I was groggy, but I remember feeling fairly okay. Abigail Evans, my consultant, came around after a while and told me that she was quite pleased with the way the operation had gone.

Abigail didn't hold anything back from me. She said my cancer had been very aggressive and she had to remove eleven lymph nodes, which was quite a lot. She also informed me that one tumour had moved out of the area and up my neck, but she was confident that she had also removed all of that bad stuff.

Mike, of course, was by my side and quite relieved that it was all over and apparently very successful. Needless to say, Mike was kept busy on the phone dealing with calls from our respective families and friends. Michael Flatley, as promised, was a regular caller, as was Niamh.

Abigail Evans came to me the following day and announced that she was extremely pleased with my progress, which gave me a great boost. Then on the Friday morning Abigail told me I could go home, which was just the best news to hear.

Vicky, my stepdaughter, and her husband, Mark, and their children, Aaron and Chloe, were there at the time. I insisted that we all stop at Harbour Heights on the way home for lunch, which we did – and, of course, I ordered a bottle of champagne!

That weekend I was full of beans, so Mike and I invited some local friends around to the house. They couldn't believe that I was up partying and dancing around, and kept urging me to sit down and rest.

The following weekend was going to be a big challenge for me with the huge auditions at Pineapple Studios in London's Drury Lane for *Michael Flatley Returns as Lord of the Dance*.

We were looking for new singers, dancers, musicians and one of the leading roles, the Little Spirit. It was too big and too late to cancel at that point as people were flying in from places like America for the chance to join the show.

As I've said before, there are no better people than the Irish dance community to rally around in times of need. My friend James McCutcheon from Scotland immediately offered to fly down and run the auditions for me.

Another friend, Hilary Joyce-Owens, who runs a lovely Irish dance school in London called Scoil Rince Céim Óir, insisted on giving up her time to work at the auditions.

Lord of the Dance tour manager Peter Mersey assured me that everything would run smoothly as he'd also be there to organise the event.

All of those offers of support took a lot of pressure off me, but I just couldn't let go. While I was so grateful to have my friends around me, I insisted on being there to conduct the process, and Mike agreed to drive me down.

'I'll sit down and I'll be good,' I promised him.

The turnout for the *Lord of the Dance* auditions that day was just massive. There were lines of people for the four or five studios that were booked for the dancers, singers and musicians.

Dance captains like Bernadette Flynn and Damien O'Kane were there, as were Ashling and Dave McCabe and Sarah Frances Smith. We had taken over all the studio, so I divided up the auditions among them. The dancers had the main studio and it was absolutely crammed.

I remember one funny incident from that day when we were auditioning for the female fiddle players in the show. We had every calibre of musician turning up for the roles, including some who had come straight out of orchestras.

One young woman arrived in with her fiddle and bow, plus a stand and sheet music. As fans will know, our fiddle players dance energetically while playing in *Lord of the Dance*.

Peter Mersey shot me a glance as if to say, 'This is going to be interesting!', when the young woman began her performance.

She played a tune beautifully and then I said, 'Now can you dance around as you are playing?'

With that, she picked up the music stand and tried to hop around with the bow, fiddle … and the music stand!

It was the most hilarious thing I'd ever seen.

I didn't dare look over at Pete because I knew that we would both explode with laughter and I'd have to be picked up off the floor. Somehow I managed to keep a straight face.

That was a full-on day, starting at 8.30 a.m. and finishing at 6 p.m. Although all my wonderful friends rallied around me to run the auditions, it was very hard for me to sit back and watch somebody else directing and before long I was hopping around the floor.

Poor Mike nearly had a heart attack over my antics.

'Hilary, will you take her out,' he pleaded.

'James, will you get her to sit down.'

That was just a week after my operation, so I had meant it when I said that while cancer was a bummer I wasn't going to let it change my life.

I wasn't going to sit in a chair moaning about it.

Of course, it was challenging at times, particularly when I started the chemo treatment. But you just have to soldier on, and you cling to the fact that eventually there will be light at the end of the tunnel.

Before my cancer was diagnosed, Mike and I had booked a villa in Cyprus where we'd intended to spend three months on holiday that summer. We had contacted some of our families and close friends and invited them to come and join us at intervals.

Peter Mersey and his wife Beverley had a home in Cyprus and we'd fallen in love with the island when we went to visit them.

We found a lovely villa through the internet, flew over for a weekend to see it, and promptly booked it for the summer. Then we got out our diary and booked in dates for our various visitors to come and chill and party with us during the three months.

As we relaxed in the sunshine at the villa that weekend and clinked our wine glasses, Mike and I were so excited about the few months of great fun that lay ahead. But, as they say, people make plans and God smiles.

Little did I know that it would be the first and last time I'd spend there.

Shortly after I started the chemo treatment, our friends James and Noreen McCutcheon were due to fly out to the villa. I couldn't make the trip, but, with great difficulty, I persuaded Mike to join them. He didn't want to leave me on my own as I was reacting in all sorts of ways to the chemo, and he only agreed to go after I arranged for some friends to come and stay with me when he was away. This put his mind at rest as he was happy that there would be someone in the house with me if I needed help.

Lord of the Dance star Bernadette Flynn had become like family to me. From the day we met our friendship grew and grew, and it was Bernadette who first came to stay with me when Mike flew out to Cyprus on the August bank holiday weekend.

I woke up at 4 a.m. as Mike was getting up to go to the airport, and immediately I felt that my throat was very sore. I decided not to say anything to Mike as he wouldn't have gone ahead with his plans.

Later that morning I drove to the airport to pick up Bernadette, and my throat was no better. I didn't mention it to Bernadette either. We had a quiet evening at home in the house, and then we both retired to bed.

During the night my throat kept me awake, so early next morning I got up and phoned an emergency line but couldn't get an answer. Bernadette came down and when she realised I wasn't well she chastised me for not calling her earlier. She then accompanied me as I drove to BMI The Harbour Hospital in Poole.

My own nurses and doctors were off as it was a bank holiday, so I was examined by staff on call, who gave me a prescription for antibiotics and sent me home.

On Monday morning I was still no better, so I rang my breast cancer nurse who spoke to the oncologist. I was then told to come to the hospital immediately. It transpired that I had some sort of fungus in my throat and it was very badly infected.

'We are admitting you to the hospital straight away,' I was informed by Lesley May, the breast cancer nurse.

So I was sent to the intensive care unit of Poole Hospital, which was just across the road from the BMI. The oncologist was very upset that I had been allowed to go home the day before.

I phoned James in Cyprus and filled him in, although I didn't tell him how bad I was. I also insisted that Mike should not be told, as he would only return home immediately. James was very uncomfortable with this, but agreed to wait until he next heard from me.

Poor Bernadette Flynn, she really hadn't expected this kind of drama on her watch. She was only staying for a couple of days and then it was my friend Brendan O'Brien's turn to fly in and take over babysitting duties.

As Bernadette flew out, Brendan landed at the airport and I had arranged for him to be picked up and taken to the hospital. My friend Hilary Joyce-Owens, who knew Brendan from the Irish dancing scene, made a two-hour journey down from London to look after him as he wasn't familiar with the area or my home.

It was just chaotic for everybody, but they were so good to me.

Mike had been due home at the end of the week, but now that I was in intensive care everyone agreed, especially James, that he had to be told. It wasn't fair on anyone keeping it from him.

As predicted, once Mike heard I was in trouble he went straight to the airport on standby. As it was high season, it wasn't easy to get a flight home, but he arrived back in Poole the evening that Brendan was leaving.

So it all worked out.

A couple of days after Mike returned from Cyprus I was discharged from hospital and quickly recovered from the incident.

* * *

I had the most wonderful, obliging, caring friends around me from the moment my cancer was diagnosed. Every day I counted my blessings. I had so much to be grateful for during that difficult time, not least being the love and devotion of my husband, Mike.

He was just an angel, the sweetest man.

I can't imagine how I would have coped if I didn't have the comfort of knowing that Mike was by my side supporting me every step of the way.

And it really was support above and beyond the call of duty when I went on the road with *Lord of the Dance*.

THE HARBOUR GIRLS

The *Michael Flatley Returns as Lord of the Dance* tour played a significant role in my recovery.

There would be many hardships involved, but I never lost my passion for the show and I believe this was ultimately very beneficial to my health.

The chemotherapy started at the same time as the rehearsals in London for the new show in which Michael was making a comeback, but I insisted on going to work every day.

My friends from the Irish dancing world outside of *Lord of the Dance* once again came to my aid with unconditional support.

One of my closest pals, Mona Roddy Lennon, was a tremendous source of emotional and practical support to me as I negotiated my way through this traumatic period in my life.

Mona and I have known each other since we were teenagers meeting up at feiseanna in Irish towns like Monaghan, Dundalk and Drogheda, as well as at the All-Irelands.

As teachers in our adult years we were the friendliest of rivals. Our lives were also bonded through our roles as adjudicators, examiners and colleagues on CLRG.

We would go on to have great craic together throughout the *Lord of the Dance* years as Mona's daughters, Ciara and Dearbhla, became lead dancers in the show. Mona and her husband, Brian, then travelled around the world to see them perform, describing themselves as 'groupies'.

Mona really was the sister I never had. We attended each other's family functions and we always knew that if ever the need arose, we would be there to support each other.

Well, that came to pass in my life and, like a true friend, Mona was by my side immediately after my cancer diagnosis and during my chemo treatment. I will never forget her kindness.

Hilary Joyce-Owens, who lived about twenty minutes from the studio, organised her own Irish dance school schedule so that she could assist me whenever I needed her.

James McCutcheon also made time in his busy life up in Glasgow to come down and lend me support.

The dance captains and leads in the show, Bernadette Flynn, Aisling and David McCabe and Tom Cunningham, made my task as smooth as possible. They knew I was coming in from chemo treatment, so every time I glanced around one of them was by my side with a glass of water.

It's the small things that mean so much.

However, I never went to work with the attitude that I was a sick person. I went in totally committed to the challenge of training up a new dance troupe for a major world tour.

Shortly after the rehearsals began, I noticed that my hair was starting to fall out. I had decided that as soon as this happened I would immediately shave the lot off. So I went to my hairdresser, Carolyn, and asked her to do the job.

I know there are many women, and men, who find their hair loss a traumatic experience, but it didn't bother me. As I glanced at my reflection in the mirror and saw the egghead staring back at me, I wasn't the least bit emotional or self-conscious. I decided to get a few wigs, particularly for special occasions, but I had no problem going out in public with a bald head or just a scarf.

Through the years dancers would mimic my reaction when I got frustrated with them in rehearsals. Apparently I would put my fingers through my hair with both hands and shake my head wildly. One day I lost my cool with the troupe at rehearsals for the new show, snatched the wig off my head in a fit of rage, and flung it across the stage. Well, jaws dropped and you could hear a pin fall. The dancers were standing around nervously eyeballing each other and glancing at the wig on the floor in the middle of them – and at that moment who walked in only Michael Flatley.

One of the dance captains immediately caught Michael's eye and indicated with a mad facial expression and a finger to the lips that now was not a good time to talk to Marie!

So Mr Flatley discreetly and briskly exited the scene.

* * *

My husband's support allowed me to go on the road around Europe with *Lord of the Dance* when the new Michael Flatley tour started. I could not have done it without Mike's total and selfless dedication to me.

The first challenge Mike had to face was overcoming his phobia of blood and needles. In order for me to travel, Mike was going to have to administer my daily injection. And I couldn't have him fainting doing it because that would be a disaster. So we got an orange and he practised on that for a while. Gradually Mike became comfortable with the procedure, and then it was time to give the real thing a shot.

And to be honest I don't know why he was so worried, as it all went fine.

After the UK and Ireland, the tour was going to take us across Germany, playing ten cities there, as well as Vienna in Austria and Zurich in Switzerland.

As I was receiving chemotherapy throughout that period, flying was too difficult for me. I did travel by plane to one or two places, but I found it very claustrophobic. There was also the hassle of getting all the medication and syringes through security; plus I had a little disc in my chest for the chemo treatment and of course that caused problems going through scanners.

So flying was a nightmare.

Instead, Mike and I made the treks across Europe, and trips back and forth to the UK for my chemo, in our car.

It was like a military operation, and we had to make sure that we brought the correct stock of medication and syringes to cover the periods we were away.

We had a small Mercedes car and I would roll the passenger seat back, cover myself with a blanket and sleep on the journeys as Mike steered us along the highways on our mission to catch boats and trains. Because you weren't allowed to stay in the car on board a boat, Mike always booked us a berth, even if we were only using it for a couple of hours.

One of the most gruelling trips was at the start of the tour. Mike and I drove from Newcastle to the port of Stranraer in south west Scotland for a ferry that would take us over to Larne in Northern Ireland, and then we'd go on to Belfast by car. We thought it was going to be an easy journey, but as we were getting close to Stranraer there was snow coming down and getting worse by the minute. By the time we arrived at the ferry it was a major snowstorm, and we got caught up in a nightmare involving a boarding queue of traffic that didn't move for fourteen hours.

We spent all of that time in the car, occasionally running the engine to try to stay warm.

At one stage Mike trotted off through the blizzard in search of food, but he found that there was nothing substantial available and he was very deflated returning with meagre bags of crisps.

That disaster in Stranraer was hardship beyond anything we imagined, but it didn't put Mike off. He was happy to continue doing the entire tour by car, boat and train if that was my wish.

And that's what we did during those winter months of 2010.

* * *

Mike remembers that when we'd arrive at the venue where *Lord of the Dance* was performing I'd jump out of the car and race to the stage. I became a different person.

I think the mindset and the approach we adopted helped me to cope with everything else that was thrown at me health-wise. And I managed to go through the six sessions of chemotherapy during all of that.

Michael Flatley was very good to me throughout that period. But I didn't make a fuss about my treatment, or talk about incidents like the time I spent in intensive care with my throat problem. It was only our families and the people who were babysitting me at the time that knew what I went through.

Michael had no idea of the effort I made to do the tour, but that was my choice. I simply told him that I would be coming and going and disappearing here and there for a few days, and Michael was happy to allow me to organise my own life around the show while I got back on my feet. And when I was with the show he booked me into the exclusive hotels where he was staying, so that I'd have the best of everything.

There were times when I had to cope with very unpleasant side effects of chemotherapy on the tour. That wasn't easy when you're on the road and away from the comforts of your own home.

When we were in Hamburg, Mike and I decided to have a wander through the Christmas market in the city to soak up the atmosphere. The German markets are just so fabulous, particularly at that time of the year. But as soon as we left the hotel I started to feel nauseous. I knew then that I was going to be violently sick and we raced back to the hotel ... where I didn't make it to the bathroom on time.

Diarrhoea was an ongoing problem as well, and that was always one of my biggest fears when I was travelling, particularly on the couple of occasions that I went by plane with the dancers and we would then transfer to a bus after we landed. I have one awful memory of having to stop the coach and get off when we were just half an hour into our journey during that period. So travelling by car and train across Europe was the better option for me.

The side effects of the drugs can be awful, and that was my experience. I think I got all of them. There were times when the medical team would suggest stopping the treatment or changing a drug, but I insisted on continuing on. I would say to myself: hopefully the next one will be easier.

At one stage I ended up with neutropaenia when my white blood cells fell dramatically. This left me exposed to bacterial infections, so I was carted back to hospital again.

My breast cancer nurse then rang Peter Mersey, the *Lord of the Dance* tour manager, and told him that the catering staff should provide liver and spinach for me whenever I was away with them.

When I went back to work, Peter took great delight in informing me that he had ordered this special diet for my meals, thinking that I would be horrified at the thought of having to eat liver and spinach. What he didn't realise, as I took equal pleasure in telling him, is that I quite like liver and spinach. So we had a laugh over that.

Then I got a blood clot, which was nothing to do with either the liver or the spinach, and I had to take a course of Warfarin.

It was one setback after another, but I persevered and got through it.

Anne Boland Kelly, a dance teacher and adjudicator in Dublin and a friend of mine going back many years, had gone through a similar cancer experience six months beforehand. Anne passed on a very good tip for coping with chemotherapy.

'You can never drink enough water,' she stressed.

And my own medical team gave me the same advice. So I was drinking gallons of water every day and it was a big help. Now I would tell anyone in the same situation to never be without a glass of water. It is an essential part of getting through the treatment.

As I said, my passion for my work definitely helped me too, and I would say to anyone facing cancer: keep as much normality in your life as you can. That was the other advice I received from my friend Anne. She would also call me regularly when I was going through the treatment to see how I was getting on, and I would moan about whatever was giving me problems. Then she'd offer me solutions from her own experience. Anne was a great help and comfort to me. Sadly we have since lost her.

After I finished the chemotherapy I had a month of rest before the radiotherapy, which I flew through without any problems.

As time went on my hair grew again. It was curly beforehand, but it came back curlier with a sort of orange colour compared to the original mousy brown. Of course, there was plenty of silver splashed throughout it as well, and I started putting colour in it when I was allowed.

Hilary, my Irish dancing friend, introduced me to a hairdresser in Chiswick called Sonia from the local Ruby B salon. Sonia uses a special hair colouring product that has no chemicals in it, which is ideal for someone who is a cancer patient. I then passed the product on to my own hairdresser and soon I was back to being a blonde again.

Well, blondes do have more fun!

My hair had started growing back just in time for some big red carpet moments when Michael Flatley launched his 3D film of *Lord of the Dance* in London's West End and on Broadway, New York, in 2011. I'm a firm believer in celebrating the good times and the special events, so I really enjoyed those nights with everyone in the company and dancers from the various schools. I took great pleasure from organising all the invitations to the Irish dancing schools in the UK and New York. We had a thousand dancers from all over New York at the Broadway premiere. Our friend, Shirley Bassey, was among the VIP guests for our big night in the West End.

* * *

In the summer of 2015, five years after I was first diagnosed with breast cancer, I got the all-clear.

The peace of mind that comes with that news is marvellous. After you get cancer, any ache or pain is a niggling worry. But I had thorough checks and all was fine.

My faith in the Sacred Heart, and in my medical team headed up by Abigail Evans and oncologist Dr. Amit Chakrabarti, had been more than justified.

I had stayed positive the whole way through my treatment, which is what you need to do, even during dark and difficult days. But I know how lucky I am to have survived my cancer because it was so far gone by the time I went to get it checked.

So, really, I was given another chance to live life and I'm so grateful for that gift.

The other positive aspect of that whole saga was the new group of friends that it brought into my life. One of them was my breast cancer nurse Leslie-May Harrison, who was a saint to me. Leslie-May has a network of people who have been through cancer and if she feels that one of her patients needs support during treatment she can link them up with someone to talk to.

When I was brought into the intensive care unit with my throat problem, Leslie-May introduced me to a lovely lady called Eve Went. Eve had been through a hard and very difficult time with her own cancer and had come out the other end. Now she takes time out of her busy life to help others as they work their way through that challenge. At the time, I found Eve's words and advice a great source of comfort and reassurance.

Leslie-May also runs a little support group called The Harbour Girls, named after the hospital. Eve brought me along to my first meeting and, again, I thought it was a wonderful service. Leslie-May had people in to talk about aftercare treatment, how to deal with different problems, advice on wigs and hair and so on. When people are vulnerable and low and struggling to fight back, this is the sort of support they need.

As Leslie-May got to know Mike and myself very well over time, she approached us one day about running a charity ball at the Haven Hotel, from which we would later form the Dorset Cancer Care Foundation.

Mike and I were delighted to get involved in organising this event with a core group that also included our new friend Eve, Sandy Cooke, who had also been through cancer treatment, and our friend Gill Emeny.

That first charity ball was a great night of fun as well as raising over £30,000 for cancer care, which was beyond everyone's expectations. We had an auction at the event where guests put in very generous bids. I volunteered a group from *Lord of the Dance* to perform a showpiece as part of the entertainment. Barry Owen and The Main Attraction were our band for the night and they filled the dance floor. The whole evening was a roaring success.

Leslie-May was so thrilled with the outcome that a seed was sown in her mind, and she later approached us about setting up a cancer foundation. My husband Mike, Pam Jeffries, Sandy Cooke and Eve Went then set about getting it started. Mike did all the paper- and legal work to secure the charitable status – and Dorset Cancer Care Foundation was eventually born.

Today, Dorset Cancer Care Foundation has charity events running every other week to raise funds, and the work that it does is invaluable to the people who benefit from it. All the money is used in a practical way to help cancer sufferers in Dorset. This includes transport to hospitals for patients who are in need of that service; babysitting and other back-up support for spouses; as well as the various day-to-day living costs that people might not otherwise be able to afford.

Dorset Cancer Care Foundation has been an opportunity for Mike and me to give back because, despite what we went through, we both appreciate our good fortune.

'Life is a combination of high points and low points, and you can't go through life without the low points,' Mike said in an interview.

'In my life, my divorce was a low point for me. But a lower point for me was Marie's cancer. We came through that together and we ended up much stronger.

'As a result of having done that, my life since then completely changed. In gratitude for Marie surviving her cancer, I became totally devoted to my work with the cancer charity in Dorset.'

As Mike says, 'It's not everybody who gets the chance to give back. We are happy and blessed to be able to do it.'

And that is the reason we also set up The Marie Duffy Foundation.

THE FOUNDATION

Irish dancing has been so good to me in life.

All through my life I was one of those lucky people who had the blessing of living to work, rather than being forced to take on employment that would give me no satisfaction other than putting food on the table and paying the mortgage. Instead, I had a job that I loved and, believe me, I always appreciated that privilege.

As old age started knocking on my door, I began thinking about giving back for all the good things in life that I had experienced through Irish dancing.

I had discussed this with my husband, Mike, one time when we were putting our affairs in order and doing our wills.

Mike, as always, was supportive and agreed that it was a very good idea. We talked about doing something for Irish dancing, but we didn't immediately set anything in motion.

Then cancer came into my life. Coming towards the end of the treatments, Mike and I were discussing how lucky I was to be seeing a positive outcome, despite the aggressive cancer having been discovered at an advanced stage.

Mike again raised our wish to give back in some way. And he came up with the idea of setting up The Marie Duffy Foundation.

It was Mike's brainchild, and he stressed: 'Okay, let's do it now and not wait until you are six feet under.'

Once I gave Mike the go-ahead, he didn't waste a moment.

Mike is a very decisive and, as I said, a very organised sort of person. He did all the spade work himself to get it off the ground, wading through the red tape, sorting out the legal side and getting it registered and approved for charitable status.

Then we set up a Board of Trustees. I proposed my friend, James McCutcheon from Scotland, as the chairman. Our friendship had grown and blossomed through Irish dancing. And, of course, he was a rock of support to me while I was battling through my cancer treatment. I also knew that when James takes anything on he gives it his full commitment. When we contacted him, James said he would be honoured to accept the position as chairman.

One of our close English friends, Eben Foggitt, a former barrister who has also worked in the British film and TV world, had no hesitation in coming on board when we extended the invitation to him.

The third person we approached to become a trustee was my nephew Len McLaughlin, who gave me away at my wedding. So, with Mike and myself, we had our five trustees.

We were also delighted when Niamh Flatley agreed to come on board as patron of The Marie Duffy Foundation. Niamh was always totally committed to everything she did through Irish dancing and I knew that she would be a great ambassador for the Foundation, and generous with her time whenever she was called upon to attend functions.

Mike and I then made a commitment to make personal yearly donations over five years to provide the Foundation with a strong financial footing, but the long-term plan is to implement fundraising activities to ensure its viability.

The initial idea behind the Foundation was to help young, aspiring dancers who didn't have the resources to follow their dream. I wanted to provide a practical back-up for those young people to achieve their ambitions through Irish culture in all of its forms.

To help us select appropriate beneficiaries of the funds, we decided to set up an Awards Selection Panel, consisting of the five trustees and its members: Sean McDonagh, Francis Curley, Terence Gillan and Myra Watters.

We were also looking for new, innovative ideas to support, so we encouraged people to apply to the Foundation by advertising through the Irish dance schools, dance magazines and on the internet.

The first focus of the Foundation in 2011 was on musicians and composers in Irish music. James McCutcheon and I came up with the idea of inviting musicians who play for all the well-known championships, or majors as we call them, to compose a tune that An Coimisiún le Rincí Gaelacha (CLRG) would recognise and put on their official list.

CLRG have a list of particular set dances that have been there since time began. While we want to keep our tradition going, we also felt it would be worthwhile adding to it. Our thinking was that anything new we do now will be tradition to the people who are around in another fifty years.

We got an excellent response to our call-out for the competition that was billed as Excellence in Irish Dance Music Composition, and then the next stage was choosing the winning tune from the selection that came in.

The Foundation had set up ties with the University of Limerick, so we had the final there in front of a live audience at a gala evening with a panel of respected judges that included James McLoughlin, Mícheál Ó Súilleabháin, Niall Keegan, Richard Griffin and Sylvan Kelly.

The unanimous winner was a young man from Glenarm, Co. Antrim, called Francis Ward, with his beautiful jig set dance music composition, 'The Vanishing Lake'.

That tune was added to the CLRG list of set dances on 1 June 2012, and is now one of the most frequently played in competitions.

It has put Francis on the map.

Francis says he drew his inspiration for the music from the legend of Loughareema (Loch an Rith Amach), or the Vanishing Lake as it is known, which lies close to Ballycastle, Co. Antrim, at the north-east tip of Ireland. It's a small lake that seems to disappear and reappear at random. The road to Ballycastle runs right through it, though the modern road sits high enough to avoid flooding.

According to legend, on the afternoon of 30 September 1898, a man called Colonel John Magee McNeille was travelling to Ballycastle, driven by a coachman in a covered wagon pulled by two horses. The road disappeared into the waters of the flooded lake as McNeille and his driver arrived at the spot, but they took the decision to wade though it. Halfway across, the horses began to get nervous as the freezing cold water reached their bellies. One of the horses reared up on its back legs and turned to the side before slipping off the road and into deeper water. The other horse had no choice but to follow, and then the carriage sank, drowning the colonel and his coachman as well as the horses.

Francis says that ever since that fateful day many people have reported seeing a phantom carriage pulled by two horses and ridden by a military man on the lonely shores of Loughareema.

His composition, 'The Vanishing Lake', remembers the Phantom horseman of Loughareema.

* * *

When 'The Vanishing Lake' was accepted by An Coimisiún, we ran a competition for dancers over the age of sixteen to create new choreography for that music. We gave the competitors lots of scope and a free hand, inviting them to come up with a freestyle piece and suitable costumes if they were going to do it show-style. It didn't have to adhere to strict competitive CLRG rules.

The crème de la crème of dancers participated in that event which was held in the City West Hotel, Dublin, at the end of the All-Ireland competitions in 2012.

The winner was a young guy called Cathal Keaney from the Celine Hession School of Dancing in Galway. Cathal went on to join *Lord of the Dance* and is now one of the new Lords.

'The Vanishing Lake set dancing competition was one of the highlights of my dancing career and I really enjoyed the whole experience,' Cathal wrote later.

'As a dancer who makes up all my own steps, this was an opportunity to be creative while competing against other senior dancers.

'I felt amazing when I was called out as the winner as I was not expecting it. Winning the competition has helped my confidence in competitive dancing and encouraged me to push myself harder and develop more intricate steps.'

The Foundation also funded Irish language scholarships that same year for two young people, Cathal O'Braonain and Niamh Nic Mhathuna.

* * *

Through the Foundation I was again reminded of the impact Michael Flatley had made, both personally and with his spectacular shows after his first *Riverdance* performance at the Eurovision Song Contest in 1994. Europe, in particular, became obsessed and absorbed with Michael Flatley. From that time on, Irish dancing classes started springing up all across the Continent. There were no borders.

In 2012, the Foundation had an application for assistance from an Irish dancing teacher called Biljana Pajic, who is based in Belgrade, Serbia, where she has established Erin's Fiddle Dance School. Biljana was seeking help from us to run a weekend workshop for over fifty dancers.

My dear friend, *Lord of the Dance* captain Bernadette Flynn, agreed to take on this project, so she flew out to Belgrade and the Foundation covered all the expenses involved.

Bernadette is such a great ambassador for Irish dancing in general, and *Lord of the Dance* in particular. Biljana later wrote how she couldn't believe her good fortune when Bernadette arrived to host their workshop.

'I started Irish dancing in 2004, and two years later established a dance group in Belgrade,' she explained.

'I could only dream about meeting and learning from one of the stars of *Lord of the Dance*. I could not imagine this at all, seriously, because in the land where I live Irish dancing isn't that famous and familiar to people.

'My dancers and I worked a lot, and achieved a lot too. Everything we've achieved until now wasn't a gift from anyone. We had no financial or any other support from any institution.

'That's the main reason why I was so delighted to find out about The Marie

Duffy Foundation. I thought it was a great opportunity for anyone who does Irish dancing and needs some kind of support. I applied hoping to have a little bit of luck, and surprisingly I got it!

'I couldn't believe what I was seeing – an offer for Bernadette Flynn to host an Irish dance workshop. The dancers were euphoric, although none of them could believe it at first. But on the 4th of May Bernadette arrived in Belgrade and the unforgettable weekend began.

'Words cannot describe how thankful we are and what this has meant to us. It's hard to find support for what we do, but this opportunity has surprised us when we least expected it, especially from someone who has never met us personally or seen us dance live. We really appreciate it.'

In 2013, the Foundation had a request from Dominique Dure, a twenty-six-year-old Irish dancing teacher in Argentina. Dominique, a native of Buenos Aires, was looking for support to travel to Ireland so that she could try for her official teaching qualification from the CLRG.

Dominique is the director of Celtic Argentina, the first ever school of Irish dance established in Argentina. It was founded in Buenos Aires by her mother, Christine, who has Irish ancestry. The popularity of the school shot up after *Riverdance* and *Lord of the Dance* performed in Buenos Aires in the year 2000.

Dominique was really passionate about Irish dancing and culture and for a long time she had harboured an ambition to become a fully qualified teacher. The Foundation was delighted to support her and cover her trip and fees for the exam. Dominique was successful on her first attempt, thus becoming the first qualified TCRG teacher in Argentina.

'This was a big achievement for me, a dream come true,' Dominique said later in an interview with *Irish America* magazine.

Today, Celtic Argentina is one of the largest Irish dance schools in South

America, and the biggest in Argentina.

Asked in the same interview why she thought Irish dancing was so popular in Argentina, where only two per cent of the population boasts Irish ancestry, it was interesting to hear Dominique's views.

'People are mainly attracted by the hard shoes,' she suggested. 'Personally I think that the sound of Irish traditional music combined with the rhythmical sound of the shoes is unique and magical.

'It's a style of dance that demands discipline, timing, elegance, rhythm and is accompanied by music that raises your spirit. Irish music is also very inviting and encourages everyone to dance, so there is always a very enthusiastic response from the public.'

The Foundation would go on to fund lectures and practical workshops at the University of Limerick, provide bursaries for final year BA students in the university, and support projects like the making of a short Irish dance film by a young woman called Aisling McFadden.

We were always on the lookout for an individual dancer, someone with a love of Irish dancing who, for whatever reason, was being deprived of the chance to pursue their passion. We wanted to put our resources behind a kid like that, and help a boy or girl to go as far as they could with their talent. And that opportunity came to me through the world of competitive dancing.

One day I was told the story of a promising young dancer who had a difficult personal life. Dancing brought this young girl great joy and it was probably her only form of escapism from the trauma that she was then dealing with in other areas of her life.

The details of her life are personal and I won't go into them. But from the moment I heard her story and saw her dance, I knew we had to help. She was a lovely young girl who had worked hard against the odds to take dancing classes and participate in the competitions. And despite the personal challenges she had to overcome, this girl had won a place at the World Championships.

However, as they were being held on the other side of the world, there was no chance of her being able to make the trip because of the expense involved.

As I said, it was individual cases like this young dancer's that we had envisaged supporting when we set up the Foundation. So I went to the board and put her case to them, and, of course, there was no problem getting approval to fund the trip, covering the girl's flights, her hotel accommodation, subsistence money and other bits and pieces.

I have to say, it was so rewarding for everyone associated with the Foundation to play a role in assisting that lovely young girl to achieve such a big dream. She couldn't stop smiling, and neither could we.

For that one case alone, it would have been worth setting up The Marie Duffy Foundation.

* * *

I'm delighted that the Foundation is now attracting huge interest and support and we believe that it has a great contribution to make to the future of Irish dance.

Whether they are complete beginners, novices or high achievers, the Foundation continues to promote ways of enhancing the skills and knowledge of dancers so that they can reach higher levels. It also provides master workshops for dance professionals.

Most recently it has funded and promoted the Aisling Awards at the World Championships to recognise the top dancers from new and developing Irish dance regions around the globe. These awards are highly sought after and have been instrumental in promoting and improving dance worldwide.

Irish dance is constantly changing and evolving, and it is the aim of the Foundation to identify and support the creative and inspirational individuals who will be at the cutting edge of dance excellence in the years ahead around the world.

As the motto of the Foundation says, *ar aghaidh linn i bhfeabhas* – we go onwards improving all the time.

ONWARDS EVER,

BACKWARDS NEVER

I've been writing this book in my seventieth year, and publishing it in a year when *Lord of the Dance* is celebrating its 21st anniversary.

Today, when I look at those numbers they don't really register with me.

Can this be true: that I'm seventy years old!

Is it really twenty years ago that I first started out on my journey with Michael Flatley in *Lord of the Dance*?

In my mind I'm still a teenager ... well, maybe a twenty-something.

My passion for life and living, dancing, partying and working hasn't waned with the passing of time.

I still get such a buzz seeing a young dance student flourish, a show come to life, and a cork pop on a bottle of champagne.

One of Ireland's greatest ever singers, Joe Dolan, who was a dear friend of mine and in whose south Dublin home I enjoyed many a great party, had a favourite expression about life.

'The future is always better than the past,' Joe would say.

Joe was a charming, smiley man who was full of fun. He was Ireland's first pop star, starting out as a showband idol in the 1960s, appearing on *Top of the Pops* in Britain, and topping the charts all over Europe with a unique voice and songs like 'Make Me An Island', 'Sister Mary' and 'Goodbye Venice Goodbye'.

But Joe wasn't the sort of guy who lived off past glories. He was always fired up with energy and enthusiasm, constantly taking up new offers, tackling modern songs and putting his own stamp on them, and literally having a ball all his life until the sands of time ran out for him.

Luck plays a part too. Joe was lucky to enjoy a great career doing something he loved: singing and performing. Away from the stage, he lived for golf.

Maybe that's the secret to staying young at heart – loving what you do.

I loved Joe's attitude to life because that's how I've always felt about it. The future is always better than the past … How right Joe was.

Until recently, I was still going at a hundred miles an hour myself and loving every minute of my work.

I never wake up in the morning and think about my age.

Act your age?

You must be joking!

My mind is still in the moment, happy to take on a new challenge.

Of course, time takes its toll on the body. Cancer takes a bigger toll, so in the last couple of years I've been advised by my friends and medical team to take my foot off the pedal and slow down. If I don't, as Abigail Evans, Eve Went and Leslie-May Harrison constantly warn me, there's trouble coming down the line.

Abigail and others remind Mike and me how lucky I am to have survived the cancer I had, because it was so far gone before I was diagnosed. They think we forget this and they urge me to step back from my work rate.

Stress is one of the worst things you can have in your life; it is a recognised cause of cancer. And even though I never thought of my work as being stressful, I'm sure it was at times. I always looked upon it as good stress, but then I'm not qualified to say that such a thing exists.

So, with the prodding of all of those good people who have my best interests at heart, I decided to cut back on my work with *Lord of the Dance*, which today employs around three hundred people. I haven't completely severed my ties and I'm available whenever my services are needed, but now I don't do the day-to-day stuff.

Michael Flatley, of course, totally understood why I had to make this decision.

When Michael danced for the last time in Ireland in March 2015, I joined him and the performers at the 3Arena. After that Dublin show, *Lord of the Dance: Dangerous Games*, where Michael received his final standing ovation amid rapturous applause in the venue where we had launched the extravaganza nineteen years earlier, he paid me a lovely tribute.

At the after-show party, in what was formerly The Point, Michael acknowledged my role in the success of *Lord of the Dance* as he announced that I was cutting back on my day-to-day responsibilities.

My ties with *Lord of the Dance* will never be fully severed, but in November

2015 I joined Michael and the troupe when we took our final bow together at the Lyric Theatre on Broadway. That was an emotional night.

I have loved every moment of my time with Michael Flatley. We've had our ups and downs, but we've come through it all with a friendship that will never be broken. It's been a big sister/little brother relationship and, naturally, like all families it didn't always run smoothly. But the important thing is, you come through the challenging times and it makes the relationship stronger.

Michael has a great heart. I've been with him for twenty years, so that says it all.

* * *

When I look back on my twenty years with the show I think about the thousands of young people I worked with in the various troupes through those couple of decades. It brings a smile to my face. At one stage we had four *Lord of the Dance* troupes running simultaneously around the world, with thirty to forty dancers in each show. Every night of the week we had at least sixty dancing on stages somewhere in the world.

Naturally, nature took its course and the young people fell in love with each other while touring with the shows. Mothers get to see their sons and daughters grow up, meet the love of their lives, and get married. Well, I had hundreds of young people doing that, so I was really blessed.

It was lovely watching all the different relationships happening and seeing the couples grow together.

Back in 1996 in Troupe 1, lead dancer Jimmy Murrihy introduced a hilarious Thirty Second Rule for young lovers. If cast members had hooked up – or 'shifted' as they used to say – on a night out, they would get the Thirty Second

Rule treatment on the bus as we travelled on to the next city the following day.

Jimmy would take the microphone on the coach, put the two unfortunate dancers in the spotlight, reveal their antics from the previous night, then give them thirty seconds to declare if they were going to make their relationship official as boyfriend/girlfriend.

This was great fun for everyone on the bus at the expense of the mortified young couple.

Many of those relationships would go on to stand the test of time, and a few probably didn't last more than thirty seconds. But in general, the couples who got together usually stayed together and went on to marry. I'm told by Jimmy Murrihy that the tradition of the Thirty Second Rule is still going strong twenty years later.

Out of those relationships came an avalanche of weddings. There were so many that I have lost track, but I was privileged to get lots of invites. It wasn't always possible for me to attend those lovely occasions due to tours and so on, but I did try to be there for the dance captains because of the personal relationships I'd built up with those individuals through working closely with them on the shows.

The very first wedding was Daire Nolan, who wasn't just a dance captain to me, but one of my great friends as well. Daire was Michael Flatley's first 'bad guy' and he danced opposite him. Catriona Hale was the lead female, and we all worked long hours and late into the night in those early days as we battled the clock in the countdown to the first opening of *Lord of the Dance*.

I remember that after one particularly stressful day I took Daire and Catriona out for a meal. We ordered a bottle of red wine and the waiter said, 'I'll leave it to breathe.'

We got totally engaged in talking, until finally Catriona said in a fit of desperation: 'Has that wine breathed yet!'

Daire and I burst into laughter.

I was on tour in America with *Lord of the Dance* when Daire's wedding came around, but I had bought the dress, the hat and the ticket home to Ireland for his big day. Daire was marrying his lovely girlfriend Carol, who wasn't one of the dancers but we all knew her well as she regularly came to the show.

The day before my flight there was an issue with the show in America and I felt that I should stay around to help resolve it. So literally at the final hour I had to make a call home to say that I wasn't going to be at the wedding. Daire, of course, completely understood the situation.

As they say, that's show business!

Today, Daire and Carol are the proud parents of three beautiful children. And that's the other lovely stage of my life because nowadays I regularly meet the next generation – the children of my dancers.

One of the weddings I did get the chance to attend was Rebecca Brady's. Rebecca was a former Inis Ealga dancer during my time there. She married Patrick Campbell, an American dancer, whom she met in *Lord of the Dance*.

I remember another lovely wedding in Donegal when local girl and *Lord of the Dance* member Tracey Smith married fellow dancer Don McCarron from England. Don was our dance captain in Las Vegas. Dancers Aisling Murphy from Cork and Dubliner David McCabe also fell in love and I was privileged to be at their wedding. They now run the Cabe Academy of Irish Dance in Dublin.

One of my fondest memories is the wedding of *Lord of the Dance* captain Bernadette Flynn, who had become like another family member to me through the years. The gorgeous young Tipperary woman found love in the show with dancer Damien O'Kane from Derry. They were well matched, as Damien is a gentleman in every respect. He was also a star dancer and he took over the lead role from Michael Flatley when he stopped performing.

I saw Bernadette and Damien start out as buddies and best friends in a little group. Then their relationship grew over the years and today, they are doting parents to a beautiful little daughter, Mia Rose.

Mike and I have a close friendship with Bernadette and Damien, and they will be a part of our lives until the day we die.

The last show wedding we had the honour of attending was that of dance captain and 'bad guy' Tom Cunningham from Dundalk and fiddle player Giada Costenaro from Italy. Their beautiful ceremony in August 2013 took place on Lake Maggiore in the elegant Italian town of Pallanza. Their guests included many dancers from *Lord of the Dance*.

We all stayed in the little resort of Stresa across the water from Pallanza and travelled to the wedding by ferry. The banquet that followed the gorgeous ceremony in a stunning church on a hill went on for hours, and my recollection is that there were around twenty courses.

It was lovely to see the smiles on the faces of Tom and Giada as their fairy-tale wedding came to life.

* * *

One day in 2006 I received a phone call from Michael Flatley while he was on holiday in the Caribbean. He was very upbeat, full of the joys … and it transpired that this had nothing to do with the beautiful weather in Barbados.

Michael called to tell me that he had just got engaged to Niamh O'Brien and they were getting married. I was thrilled for both of them.

Niamh was also like a daughter to me, as I had known her since she was just three years old. Her mum, Monica, used to refer to me as 'Niamh's second mother' because I was on the road with her when she joined our shows.

Niamh had been a lovely child to teach when she first started dancing in my classes. She then really impressed me in her adult life, both on a personal and professional level. She was always very quiet and serious and totally committed to her dancing and to the show. She was a perfectionist in the way she trained and prepared for her performance.

I never remember Niamh getting injured and that's because she did everything by the book, including 'Marie's warm-up exercises'.

While she was working in Las Vegas a vacancy for a dance captain came up, and I then appointed Niamh to that position. She did a great job. She was very good with the girls in the company and kept in regular contact to update me when I was back in England.

In 2005, Michael launched a new dance show called *Celtic Tiger*, which explored the history of the Irish people and Irish emigration to America through dance. It was my favourite show because I particularly love the dance numbers in it. Even today I still put on the *Celtic Tiger* DVD and I enjoy watching it.

When we were starting up *Celtic Tiger* I asked Niamh to be the dance captain and to work alongside me. I was staying in Dublin's Gresham Hotel during that period. After a long, hard day of rehearsals, Niamh and a couple of the other girls would come back at night to my room and we'd work on the new dance numbers for the next day.

Niamh always gave her time above and beyond the call of duty.

When Michael and Niamh started dating it didn't come as a big surprise to me. I knew that Niamh adored Michael and I could see the chemistry between them. And when the romance finally blossomed it was lovely to watch it develop and grow.

In October, 2006, Michael and Niamh were married at the local church near his palatial home in Fermoy, Co. Cork. It really was like the wedding of a prince and princess that day with all the locals lining the streets of the town and giving the couple a big warm welcome as they arrived. There was cheering and clapping from the gathering, with people standing on walls and fences and hanging out of windows to catch a glimpse of the bride and groom.

Even the notorious Irish weather blessed the happy couple with sunshine for their big day.

Michael and his brother, Patrick, arrived at the church in a BMW convertible with the roof down. The groom's beaming smile left no one in doubt about his joy at marrying Niamh.

The church ceremony was so beautiful and understated, and I had the honour of doing one of the readings.

Afterwards, Michael and Niamh walked down the aisle and out into the sunshine as man and wife to more loud cheers and shouts of good wishes from the waiting crowd.

Then it was back to Michael's (and now Niamh's) magnificent mansion, Castlehyde, which had once been the ancestral home of Ireland's first president, Douglas Hyde. Michael had lovingly restored the house to its former glory, and he threw open the doors to all the wedding guests on that special day.

The celebrations in Castlehyde were just like a family gathering, as guests roamed through the halls and rooms, mingling and chatting, and enjoying lovely food, wine and Guinness on tap.

And, in typical Irish fashion, the party continued into the early hours of the morning with a great music session headed up by none other than Irish traditional supergroup The Chieftains, with Michael playing the flute in the middle of them.

Later, Michael and Niamh would be blessed with the birth of their son, Michael Jnr.

A truly happy ending to their lives in dancing.

* * *

I will never leave Irish dancing while blood still runs through my veins. And it seems that Irish dancing doesn't want to leave me. After twenty years, I have been lured back into the world of competitive dancing as a teacher with the London-based school, Céim Óir, run by my friend Hilary Joyce-Owens.

Hilary comes from the west of Ireland – born in Mayo, she grew up in Galway, but if both counties were in an All-Ireland final she'd be shouting for Mayo! – and I first came in contact with her when she was about thirteen years old.

I remember judging Hilary in a competition held in Galway at that time and she really impressed me. For some reason, her name, Hilary Joyce, stuck in my head and I never forgot it. Then she just seemed to disappear off the scene. For years after I would be looking out for this kid who had impressed me, but she didn't seem to be around.

It transpired that Hilary had emigrated to England after finishing her education and had continued her Irish dancing with a London-based school.

She later took her Irish dancing teacher's exam and opened up her own school, Céim Óir, which brought me into contact with her again. I became friendly with her, but only casually. We'd exchange pleasantries and small talk whenever we'd meet on the scene.

After *Lord of the Dance* was launched I found myself in London a lot of the time, and Hilary would come to the shows. Then, when she heard that I had been diagnosed with cancer, she called me up and offered to help in any way she could.

As I mentioned earlier, Hilary was one of the people who supported me when I was rehearsing a new *Lord of the Dance* troupe in London shortly after I had my mastectomy. It was during this time that our friendship deepened and from then on we were in touch all the time.

When I first talked about stepping back from my work with *Lord of the Dance*, Hilary asked if I would be interested in doing some mentoring with the young dancers at her Céim Óir school. I didn't immediately commit to anything. Later, when I was mulling it over, I wasn't sure that I could go back into competitive dancing again and cope with the pressures and emotions that go with the scene.

So I put it on the long finger.

In 2014 I asked Hilary if she would work with me on the creation of a big production for the opening ceremony of the World Championships in London that year. I wanted to do something that had never been done before and make it exciting and entertaining for everyone.

My vision was for a showpiece that would have the wow factor, and Hilary jumped on board to help me bring it to life.

Hilary's husband, Barry, and his band, The Main Attraction, are one of the top groups in the world of corporate entertainment on the Irish circuit in Britain. Barry, who originally comes from Belfast, agreed to be the musical director for the production, creating the appropriate tunes for the different elements of the show.

I laid out a blueprint for the event, and then the next step was to get all the London dancers, and especially the teachers and adjudicators, to participate in the show. I was thrilled with the response. They all immediately jumped in with great enthusiasm.

We had intended our show-style opening ceremony to be a surprise, but, of course, with dancers and teachers involved it was impossible to get them to hold their whist, as we say, and the word got out.

On opening day, there was a huge buzz around the place and the auditorium was packed to capacity, with a queue of people outside the door hoping for individuals to give up their seats.

There were over sixty nations participating in the World Championships, so we had a parade of flags with the southern dancers each representing a nation. Barry's music was the soundtrack to that display, with a suitable tune for each country. I had also asked Barry to write and record an anthem for those World Championships, and that was played every day throughout that marvellous week.

It was also a great honour to have the participation of Michael Flatley and his wife, Niamh, in the opening ceremony. Their presence created a big buzz and the crowd just loved them.

Brian McEnteggart, a former *Lord of the Dance* dancer, composed a hilarious monologue on the World Championships, which was recited during the evening's entertainment by Francis Curley.

The other big hits on the night included a light-hearted parody sketch with a London theme, a pledge of allegiance for dancers, adjudicators and musicians, and a show-style dance performance by the younger teachers.

They brought the house down.

That was April 2014, and the following month I decided to start working with Hilary in her Céim Óir classes after she again asked me if I would be interested in coming in the odd time to do some mentoring. As I was living in Dorset, a couple of hours from London, I offered to do two days with

Céim Óir every fortnight.

Hilary and I get on so well. It's like we've known each other all our lives. She is a beautiful young woman in every sense: she's very pretty with blonde hair, hazel eyes and a vivacious personality. I liked her ethics and the way she ran her classes. She's a great organiser with attention to detail and she has a natural rapport with young people.

But, despite our great relationship, I have to admit that I was very apprehensive about going back into the competitive world after twenty years away from it working on the international stage with *Lord of the Dance* and all of Michael Flatley's spin-off shows.

However, it was too big a challenge to turn down, so I stepped back into the inferno. And I wasn't long in the door of Céim Óir when I felt right at home. I quickly became inspired by the dedication of the pupils and their parents and gradually I got more and more connected, involved and attached to the youngsters – and the two days multiplied.

Every teacher and dancer and class's aim is to come home from the World Championships with as many globes as possible. At the 2015 championships in Montreal our Céim Óir dancers surprised themselves. They won their first céilí team championship, which meant that the dancers received the coveted globes and were placed on the podiums. Hilary's own daughter, Ella Owens, came third, and a young lad called Josh Ruddock won second place in the men's.

That created so much excitement in Céim Óir that all of the dancers wanted to do the journey for the 2016 World Championships in Glasgow, to see how far they could go. Sarah Cooney-Nutley was a senior dancer in her last year and her determination, dedication, commitment and loyalty were so infectious that I became totally engrossed in working with her and the rest of the dancers over the year.

They were enjoying it and I was enjoying it.

It was just so exciting.

And I got the fire in my belly again.

The world of competitive dancing is a roller coaster of highs and lows. It's so subjective in competition that there are going to be down days as well as up days. I always tell dancers that they can't expect to go through the World Championships on either total highs or total lows.

Our week at the 2016 World Championships started off on a great high. Ella Owens got a second place, which was a huge personal achievement to move up into that position over the year. The middle of the week brought some lows, but then on Easter Sunday we were back on top of the roller coaster, with the two céilí teams both taking globes.

Then came the ultimate high when Josh Ruddock achieved his dream of making the number one spot.

Looking at the beaming face of Josh up on the winner's podium was such an emotional experience for me.

I never expected to be back on stage as one of the teachers of a new World Champion after a break of twenty years … and at the age of seventy!

* * *

In my seventieth year I'm on the move again, relocating from the gorgeous Poole suburb of Canford Cliffs to an apartment in a lovely little town called Gerrards Cross.

There are several reasons for this latest upheaval in our lives, but first let me go back to Canford Cliffs, the truly stunning area where Mike and I set up home together after we got married.

When we lived in Three Legged Cross we'd often take a scenic drive out that way, up along the eastern edge of Poole Harbour. Canford Cliffs is a sleepy area with lovely little tree-lined roads and beautiful homes. It is linked to Sandbanks, a peninsula of just half a square mile of golden sand that is one of the most expensive areas in the world to buy a house.

Sandbanks has only seventy or so homes around the edge of the peninsula, so they are the most sought-after. And the forty or so houses that have direct access to Poole Harbour go for serious money. I've seen price tags of £13 million!

Sandbanks is not a haunt of A-list actors or pop stars, but more of football managers, including Harry Redknapp.

With those kind of prices, Sandbanks was not for us, but Canford Cliffs won our hearts. The area was originally designed to be residential, with a church and village hall, but few commercial buildings. The Canford Cliffs Society still works to preserve those goals, so there are few businesses and no industry in the area.

After we got married, Mike sold his cottage and we were then living together in my house next door. One weekend when Mike was away I took a drive around Canford Cliffs with my nephew-in-law Len and I started admiring houses, including a row of four similar new ones on a little road quite close to the sea.

When Mike came home, I suggested that we should go and have a look around that area together to see if there was anything we both fancied.

We then took a trip around Canford Cliffs, checking out what was on offer, but not spotting anything suitable that we could agree on. Before going home I remembered the row of new houses I had seen with Len, so Mike agreed to call by, although I think his patience was well on the way to running out at this stage.

The four houses were slightly different in size, and I immediately fell in love with one of them. However, when we contacted the estate agent I was disappointed to learn that it had already been sold. We were then told that the house at the end, which was the biggest one on the row, was still available.

We got a viewing and when we walked through the door it was still a work in progress. A lot of the interior hadn't been completed, but we both loved it. A house chooses you, as they say. Before we left we were doing a deal with the estate agent.

And soon after that our home at Three Legged Cross went on the market.

We settled into Canford Cliffs as if it had always been a part of our lives. As we expected, it was a heavenly place to live. We both realised how fortunate we were to have such a good life in that part of the world.

Apart from our lovely home, the main attraction for both of us was our proximity to the sea, which was just a short stroll down the hill from our house. There is a beautiful sandy beach with a great prom for long walks. We really were in heaven.

As time slipped by, Mike and I both established great new friendships with people in the area. Our home on the hill played host to many an enjoyable and memorable dinner party. It was also in Canford Cliffs that Mike came into his own as the king of the barbeque. He always enjoyed surprising our guests with new barbeque recipes on balmy summer evenings.

I know I can depend on Mike to provide a top-class meal whenever we have a gathering. I remember when our friends Chris Thomas and Eve Went were celebrating their sixtieth birthdays, a gang of us went off together to the Turks and Caicos Islands in the Caribbean for a week of fun. Sue and her husband, Chris, have a fabulous home sitting right on the beach in that idyllic part of the world.

It was decided that each guest would take turns to do a daily lunch throughout the week. Naturally it was Mike who stepped up to the challenge in our couple and he cooked one of his signature dishes, paella. Beforehand, Mike took me on an expedition to the local market to stock up on all the essential items that go into paella. He's meticulous about sourcing his ingredients – I suppose that's the engineer in him. Mike does a mean paella that guests just love; even those who are not fans of that dish seldom resist the one that my husband makes.

When Mike celebrated his seventieth birthday three years ago, I offered him the choice of a Rolex watch or an outdoor state-of-the-art barbeque kitchen for his present. With his passion for outdoor cooking, Mike opted for the kitchen. And when it arrived he was like a child with a new toy on Christmas morning. Our families and friends have ever since enjoyed the benefits of that gift.

So why take the major decision to move from our lovely village of Canford Cliffs at this stage of our lives? It is for a combination of reasons.

Firstly, we're getting on in years, so we felt it was time to downsize from our large, two-storey house and move to more manageable apartment living.

A tragic accident had also unsettled us in the last couple of years when our next-door neighbour died after falling down her stairs. That scared us, so the stairs were becoming an issue, particularly as Mike has arthritis.

Ultimately, where you live is defined by the people in your life, rather than bricks and mortar. In the last couple of years a lot of our close friends moved on from Canford Cliffs, so that also had a bearing on it.

But, as with everything in my entire life, the main reason is to do with Irish dancing. I am thoroughly enjoying working with Hilary and her dancers and teachers in Céim Óir, and it made more sense to be based in London rather than doing the two-hour commutes, particularly as I used to drive home on my own at night.

Once the decision was made, Mike immediately set about finding a suitable location and apartment. He really is a very proactive person, and age certainly hasn't slowed him down. And, of course, Mike has been used to moving home all his life, so it's not the least bit daunting for him.

He never gets emotionally attached to a house.

Before I had time to draw my breath, Mike had found us an ideal apartment in Gerrards Cross, a town which spans the foothills of the Chiltern Hills and land on the right bank of the River Misbourne. Gerrards Cross has a close association with popular culture. Stanley Kubrick filmed some of the exteriors of his 1962 film, *Lolita*, in the town. St Hubert's House there has been used as a filming location for several TV series, including *Inspector Morse* and *The Professionals*.

For Mike and me, Gerrards Cross ticks all the boxes for our future plans. Our apartment is a short walk to the local train station, and the train journey into the centre of London is just eighteen minutes. We also plan to to spend more time abroad in sunny climes, and Heathrow Airport is just a fifteen-minute drive away.

Since moving into the apartment we have started to turn it into our home. It's a big change in terms of reduced space, but we are happy that we've made the right decision. We both fell in love with the apartment and the location on our first visit one weekend. We were informed that there was a lot of interest in it from other parties, so we bought it on the spot.

The next challenge was to downsize our possessions and begin the big move. I wasn't looking forward to all the effort that was going to entail.

And I certainly hadn't factored in doing it with a major injury.

* * *

Glasgow's Royal Concert Hall was the venue in February 2016 for the 32nd All-Scotland Championships in Irish Dancing, run by my friends James and Noreen McCutcheon.

James and I are very supportive of each other as friends in Irish dancing, so I had travelled up to Glasgow to do some stage management and to compère some of the championships for him.

On the Friday morning we had completed two hours of the competitions by 10 a.m., so it was time for a break.

So far, so good; everything was going smoothly.

As we got set to resume the competitions, I picked up a wireless microphone and swivelled on the spot to go back on stage. In that split second the toe of my shoe stuck in my silk trousers and got caught in the carpet. I went crashing to the ground and landed on my shoulder, which took the entire weight of my body.

I had protected the microphone in my hand instead of saving myself during the fall. And I knew instantly that I was in serious trouble.

The pain was excruciating.

A nurse called Breeda Ojo, whose children were competing in the championships, immediately rushed to my aid. A taxi was organised and Breeda accompanied me to the local hospital.

On that journey I became intimately acquainted with every bump and pothole on the roads and streets of Glasgow city. I have been through cancer, but I never endured such pain in my whole life as I did on that trip.

We were booked into the Carlton George Hotel in Glasgow for the weekend, and my husband Mike had stayed behind that morning to do some administration work for the charities we're involved in. He was then shocked to receive a call telling him that I was now on my way to hospital after a nasty fall in the venue.

The news at the hospital wasn't good: there were three breaks in the head of the humerus. Basically, my shoulder was banjaxed. The pain was literally unbearable. But there wasn't a lot that they could do, except stick me in a sling.

We flew back home to London on the Monday and I went to my local hospital to continue being monitored before they made a decision on surgery. That was eventually the course of action and a plate was inserted in my right shoulder.

Apart from the horrendous torture that goes with such an injury, equally frustrating was the total loss of my independence. I couldn't do a single thing for myself.

If Mike hadn't already earned sainthood up to that point, he did then. The care, dedication and loyalty I received from him in the weeks after my accident epitomises what true love is. Mike had to wash me, dry me, dress me, feed me and nourish me every day. It was a twenty-four-seven commitment from him.

What I went through with the cancer was life-threatening, but I never envisaged the pain, trauma and disability that would result from a simple fall.

We take so much for granted.

That happened in the middle of our move from Poole to Gerrards Cross, just to throw a little extra stress into the pot for us. What can you do? You just keep going.

However, I don't know how I would have got through it if I didn't have Mike to mind me.

Sadly, my injury prevented me from taking up Michael Flatley's invitation of a trip to Las Vegas the following month to be by his side as he took his final bow at the Colosseum in Caesars Palace on St Patrick's Day.

Michael, of course, was genuinely upset and concerned when he heard about my injury.

Vegas would have been the perfect end to our twenty years on the road together. We had enjoyed some of our greatest moments during the early days of *Lord of the Dance* in Vegas.

Michael has left the stage, but *Lord of the Dance* goes on with new talent.

As the curtain came down on his dancing career for the final time, Michael told the *Review Journal*: 'I've got some terrific talent coming up now. They're just dynamite. The audiences are going crazy for them; the women love them.'

It reminds me of someone from twenty years ago!

Like myself, Michael said that what gives him the most satisfaction when he looks back is the careers he has created for young dancers.

'For twenty years I've kept thousands of young dancers working and travelling the world,' he said. 'That's a dream come true for me, giving these young people a chance to earn money doing what they dream of.'

Michael leaves the stage with his legend established in history as one of the world's greatest ever dancers.

But there has been a huge personal price to be paid for putting his body through the kind of trauma Michael's has endured as he pushed himself beyond the limits on the road to superstardom.

'I've wrecked my body with dance,' he admits. 'Every morning my poor wife, Niamh, has to witness me spending the first few minutes of the day trying to straighten my back and push my legs to start working.

'I can't say I wasn't warned, but I can't say I haven't loved every minute of putting myself into this state.'

For Michael, the show will go on behind the scenes. And, as I said, I'll be there whenever he needs me.

I guess it's like a family: although you step back, you don't divorce yourself from them entirely.

* * *

I have lived my own life through Irish culture, dance and music and whenever I talk about Ireland I refer to it as 'home'.

Ireland will always be home to me, but I love my life in England with Mike.

For a period during what they called the 'Celtic Tiger' years in Ireland, Mike and I had our own apartment in Dublin.

We were down at the World Championships in Killarney, Co. Kerry, one time, and Mike was flicking through a property supplement in the *Irish Independent* when he spotted apartments for sale near The Point venue in the docklands.

'Look at these apartments – it would be great to have a base here,' Mike said.

At that time we were over and back to Ireland quite a bit, and we travelled by boat to take the car. It did make sense to have somewhere to call home while we were in Dublin. So we made an appointment to go and see the apartments, and we travelled up from Killarney.

We ended up buying the penthouse, which was a lovely two-bed apartment overlooking the River Liffey. That became our Dublin home for a few years, and I decorated it with a full Irish theme. There were pictures of Irish poets on the walls, a portrait of Molly Malone, scenes from the 1916 Rising and a framed copy of The Proclamation.

Aunt Em would have been proud of me!

Mike loved it all.

Before we got together, Mike hadn't been to Ireland since 1966 when he came over and did a car trip on a holiday around the country with a couple of friends.

His busy career had taken him to other parts of the world throughout his life, so he didn't know what he was missing in the intervening years. He loved the time he spent at our Dublin apartment before we eventually sold it due to our commitments in the UK.

Mike is made for Ireland, being such a sociable person. He has always said to me that Irish people are so friendly and such good company. So, after hitching up with me, I guess that was a bonus for him.

We might have come from different cultural backgrounds, but it has never been an issue between us.

I've been blessed to find Mike Pask, even if it did take us forever to get together. But it was worth the wait – for both of us.

Writing this book has made me realise that, despite the heartaches that come with living, mine has been a charmed life.

I've had incredible experiences.

But I hope the best is yet to come.

As my old pal Joe Dolan said, 'The future is always better than the past.'

Or, as my dear friend Laverne Showalter used to say: 'Onwards ever, backwards never!'

Keep on dancing.